FOSSIL
HUNTING

The expert guide to finding and identifying
fossils and creating a collection

FOSSIL
HUNTING

Featuring more than 400 detailed
photographs, maps and fossil illustrations

STEVE PARKER

southwater

This edition is published by Southwater, an imprint of Anness Publishing Ltd, Hermes House, 88–89 Blackfriars Road, London SE1 8HA; tel. 020 7401 2077; fax 020 7633 9499

www.southwaterbooks.com; www.annesspublishing.com

If you like the images in this book and would like to investigate using them for publishing, promotions or advertising, please visit our website www.practicalpictures.com for more information.

UK agent: The Manning Partnership Ltd; tel. 01225 478444; fax 01225 478440; sales@manning partnership.co.uk
UK distributor: Grantham Book Services Ltd; tel. 01476 541080; fax 01476 541061; orders@gbs.tbs-ltd.co.uk
North American agent/distributor: National Book Network; tel. 301 459 3366; fax 301 429 5746; www.nbnbooks.com
Australian agent/distributor: Pan Macmillan Australia; tel. 1300 135 113; fax 1300 135 103; customer.service@macmillan.com.au
New Zealand agent/distributor: David Bateman Ltd; tel. (09) 415 7664; fax (09) 415 8892

Publisher: Joanna Lorenz
Editorial Director: Helen Sudell
Project Editor: Melanie Hibbert
Production Controller: Helen Wang
Consultant: John Cooper (Booth Museum, Brighton)
Contributors: Vivian Allen, Julien Divay, Ross Elgin, Carlos Grau, Robert Randell, Jeni Saunders and Matt Vrazo
Book and Jacket Design: Nigel Partridge and Balley Design
Artists: Andrey Atuchin, Peter Barrett, Stuart Carter, Anthony Duke, Samantha J. Elmhurst and Denys Ovenden

ETHICAL TRADING POLICY
Because of our ongoing ecological investment programme, you, as our customer, can have the pleasure and reassurance of knowing that a tree is being cultivated on your behalf to naturally replace the materials used to make the book you are holding. For further information about this scheme, go to www.annesspublishing.com/trees

Previously published as part of a larger volume, *The World Encylcopedia of Fossils and Fossil Collecting*

Publisher's Note:
Although the advice and information in this book are believed to be accurate and true at the time of going to press, neither the authors nor the publisher can accept any legal responsiblity or liability for any errors or omissions that may be made nor for any inaccuracies nor for any harm or injury that comes about from following instructions or advice in this book.

PICTURE ACKNOWLEDGEMENTS
Note: t=top; b=bottom; m=middle; l=left; r=right. Further detail of image is given where position on page might be difficult to clarify.

Artworks
Andrey Atuchin 35br (Giganotosaurus); Peter Barrett 10bl (Jurassic scene); 28b (freshwater scene); 29 (panel); 29br (dinosaur tracks); 34mr (Baryonyx); 52br (Pteranodon); 63bl (Nautilus); 63 (panel, left, modern coelacanth); Stuart Carter 32bl (Iguanodon); Anthony Duke 13 ('recording geological time'), 22b ('how a fossil forms'); 29br (dinosaur footprints map); 65tr (human migration map). All panel reconstructions as credited below; Denys Ovenden all artworks on pages 62–3 except for Nautilus and modern coelacanth (see Peter Barrett, above); 65 (panel). Reconstructions of fossils appearing in the panels on pages 68–95 were drawn by Anthony Duke, except for 95b which was drawn by Samantha J. Elmhurst www.livingart.org.uk

Photographs
The following photographs are © iStockphoto: 6bl, 7t, 7b. The following photographs are © Corbis (www.corbis.com): 8/9, 12 (panel), 14tr, 14bl, 18bl, 21tr, 26tr, 27tl, 30tl, 30tr, 31 (panel), 34bl, 35tr, 36tr, 37tr, 38tr, 45tr, 55tr, 55br, 56tl, 56bl, 57tr, 57mr, 58tr, 58mr, 61bl, 61br, 63tr, 64bl, 64b. The following photographs are © Natural History Museum Picture Library, London (www.piclib.nhm.ac.uk): 6tr, 11tr, 16tr, 16bl, 24bl, 25tl, 30br, 31tl, 31tr, 32tl, 32tr, 33tl, 33tr, 33 (panel), 34tr, 36bl, 37 (panel), 38tr, 38bl, 39bl, 39 (panel), 40tr, 42bl, 43tl, 43bl, 43 (panel), 44/5 (all photographs except 45tr), 51tr, 51br, 51 (panel), 53br, 53 (both images in panel), 54tr, 56tr, 57 (panel), 58bl, 60tr, 60bl, 61tr, 61mr, 61 (panel), 62bl, 63tl, 64t, 69t, 74, 75b, 78t, 78b, 81t, 81b, 81 (panel), 87 (panel), 92t, 94t, 95t. The following photographs are © NHPA (www.nhpa.co.uk): 66/7, 72 (panel), 73 (panel), 74 (panel). 33bl (Crystal Palace dinosaurs) © Mary Evans Picture Library (www.maryevans.com). The following photographs are © The Science Photo Library, www.sciencephoto.com: 94b. The following photographs are © Anness Publishing Ltd, and feature specimens from the following locations: Museum of Wales, Cardiff, Wales 11bl (all images except 11tr), 20tr (claw and tooth), 21tl (bivalves), 21 (panel), 21mr (leaf), 22tr (trilobite), 23 (panel), 24ml (ammonite), 25 (panel), 25b (fish), 27bl (frog skull), 28tr (vertebrae), 41br, 42tr, 43br, 46 (panel), 47tl, 47tr, 49tl, 49 (panel), 50tl, 50tr, 50b (shoal), 52tl (display), 52tr (toe and hoof), 68t, 68b, 69b, 70/1 (all photographs), 72b, 73t, 75t, 76b, 77b, 79b, 80t, 83t, 84t, 85 (all photographs except 85tr), 86t (both photographs of Lopha), 87 (all photographs of Gryphea except largest in centre), 88/9 (all photographs except 88t), 90bl, 91 (panel), 93 (moulted feathers and bird eggs), 95b. Booth Museum of Natural History, Brighton & Hove City Council, England 10tm (trilobite), 20bl (fish), 26ml (fern), 29tb (pond snails), 46tr, 47ml, 47mr, 48 (all photographs except 48tr), 49br, 50ml, 50mr, 50b, 59br, 59 (panel), 79t, 79m, 82t, 82 (panel), 85 (top photograph of Calymene), 86b, 87t (largest photograph of Gryphea in centre), 88t, 90/1 (all photographs except Hybodus, bl), 93bl (pseudofossil). Manchester Museum, England 18tm (sponge), 24tr (chain coral), 63bl (nautiloid), 76t, 83b, 84b

Additional photography credits
Sequoia fossil p27 (panel) © Rich Paselk, Natural History Museum, Humboldt State University, CA, USA. Dorothy Hill p35 (panel) © The Physical Sciences and Engineering Library, University of QLD, Australia. Kings Canyon p53bl © Amy-Jane Beer/Origin Natural Science. Thanks to Roy Shepherd for jacket images (back bm, br and front main) and p6br © www.discoveringfossils.co.uk

CONTENTS

INTRODUCTION

Fossils have been treasured since ancient times. Long ago, people gathered these strangely shaped lumps of stone for many purposes – as objects of worship, signs of their worldly wealth and power, evidence of their god's handiwork, or simply as beautiful and elegant items to display and admire.

Fossil collectors of the ancient world could not have understood how their curiosities were formed. They could not know the enormous contribution of fossils to the development of modern scientific knowledge, about the Earth and the living things that have populated it through time. Had they understood the significance of fossils, they might well have been even more amazed at what they had collected.

More than 2,000 years ago in Ancient Greece, natural philosophers such as Aristotle mused on fossils and their origins. Some explanations were inorganic – fossils were nature's sculptures, fashioned by wind, water, sun, ice and other non-living forces. Some explanations were supernatural – fossils were the work of mythical beings and gods, placed on Earth as examples of their omnipotent powers. Aristotle himself described how fossils developed or grew naturally within the rocks, from some form of seed which he called 'organic essence'.

Below: Reconstructions from fossils of dinosaurs such as the famous Tyrannosaurus rex *continue to fascinate.*

In the 1500s, firmer ideas took root. In 1517 Italian physician-scientist Girolamo Frascatoro was one of the first on record to suggest that fossils were the actual remains of plants, creatures and other organisms or living things. In 1546 German geologist Georgius Agricola coined the word 'fossil', but not as we now understand it. His 'fossils' were almost anything dug from the ground, including coal, ores for metals and minerals, and what he believed to be rocks that just happened to be shaped like bones, teeth, shells and skulls. In 1565 Swiss naturalist Konrad von Gesner's works contained some of the first studied drawings of fossils. However, like Agricola, von Gesner believed that they were stones which, by chance, resembled parts of living things.

A fashion for fossils began in the 1700s in Europe. Wealthy folk established home museums where they displayed fossils, stuffed birds and mammals, pinned-out insects, pressed flowers and so on. Around 1800, scientists began to ponder more deeply on the true origins of fossils. It was suggested that they may indeed be the remains of once-living things. But as

Below: A palaeontologist discovers ancient ammonite fossil remains within a rock on the Jurassic Coast of England.

Below: This shoebox-sized fossilized tooth belonged to a brown woolly mammoth.

all life had been made by God, and God would not allow any of his creations to perish, fossils could not actually be from extinct organisms. They must be from the types of living things which are still alive today.

Famed French biologist Georges Cuvier broke ranks. He studied the huge, well-preserved skull of a 'sea lizard' that looked like no living reptile, which he named *Mosasaurus*. Cuvier also examined fossil mammoth bones and saw their differences from those of living elephants. His new explanation was that these fossils were the remains of creatures that had indeed become extinct – in the Great Flood of Noah's time, as described in the Bible. As more and more varied fossils were dug, from deeper rock layers, the explanation grew into the story of Seven Floods. Each deluge saw a great extinction of living things.

Above: Museum collections and exhibitions, especially those with well-designed displays and reconstructions, are excellent places to learn more about fossils and their origins.

Then God re-populated the Earth with a new, improved set of organisms.

In 1859 English naturalist Charles Darwin's epic work *On The Origin Of Species* brought the idea of evolution to the fore. Fossils fitted perfectly into this scientific framework. Indeed they were used as major evidence to support it. In the struggle for survival, species less able to adapt to the current conditions died out, while better-adapted types took over. However the process never reaches steady state or an end point, since conditions or environments change through time – forcing the organisms to evolve with them. This explains not only the presence of fossils in the rocks, but also why these fossils exhibit changes over time.

Today the origins of fossils are well documented. And fossils are central to the story of Life on Earth – from the earliest blobs of jelly in primeval seas, to shelled creatures that swarmed in the oceans, enormous prehistoric sharks, the first tentative steps on land, the time of the giant dinosaurs, and the rigours of the ice ages with their woolly mammoths and sabre-toothed cats. A recent spate of discoveries now allows us to trace the origins of our own kind, back to ape-like creatures in Africa several million years ago. Yet, in addition to this scientific basis, we can still regard fossils as ancient people did – with wonder and appreciation of their natural beauty, while holding a part of Earth's history in our hands.

This following pages are packed with everything the budding fossil collector needs to know as they embark on this compelling and rewarding pastime. The first section guides you through the stages of evolution, explains how fossils form and the major habitats in which they are most commonly unearthed. You'll discover how to plan and execute a dig, and learn the best techniques for cleaning, identifying and storing any finds. A stunning visual directory of over 50 plant and animal species will inspire you to get collecting.

Left: This dinosaur footprint was preserved in the rock at the Dinosaur Valley State Park in Glen Rose, Texas, in the United States.

FOSSILS AND FOSSIL-HUNTING

Fossils are usually described as parts of living things which died long ago, and were preserved in the rocks, turned to stone. The processes of fossilization can happen in different ways, as described over the following pages. But they all share three main features.

First, the original objects preserved are from all kinds of living organisms – not only animals, but plants, fungi and even microbes. Second, the process takes a very long time – at least many thousands of years. Indeed, the majority of fossils are millions of years old. Third, most fossils are not the actual substances and materials from those once-living organisms. Fossilization gradually replaces living or organic matter with inorganic minerals and crystals. So, in general, a fossil is a lump of stone or rock. However its shape is taken from that of the original organism. This is summarized in the phrase 'bone to stone'.

Fossils themselves are fascinating, but many people gain even greater enjoyment by searching for them. It involves the thrill of the chase, and anticipation of an exciting new discovery. Fossil-hunting is an active outdoor pursuit, in the fresh air amid often beautiful scenery. It allows us to expand our basic understanding of geology and biology, from the way landscapes form and erode, to the shapes of snail shells and sharks' teeth.

Fossil-hunting always produces results. For some, the greatest satisfaction lies in creating a well-thought-out display. For others, it's about making a contribution to local or even national museums and to existing paleontological knowledge. For the few who come across a spectacular find, the attraction may even lie in fame and fortune.

Left: Rocks within the Earth's crust are subject to dramatic movements over a very long period of time, crumbling and slipping into the oceans or being raised into towering mountain ranges. These footprints were originally made by a carnivorous dinosaur upon an ancient Cretaceous shoreline, but have since been lifted, over millions of years, to form part of a near-vertical fault in the Andes. The palaeontologist measuring the stride of the creature has had to overcome some difficulty in access to record this information.

FOSSILS THROUGH TIME

Fossils trace the evolution of life from the tiniest, simplest scraps of living matter, to huge and complex creatures like dinosaurs, whales and mammoths. It is a very long story, spanning billions of years, with many surprising events along the way.

The oldest known fossils are microscopic shapes in rocks dating back more than 3,500 million (3.5 billion) years. That's 3,500,000,000 years – a very long time. In fact it's more than two-thirds of the time that our planet has been in existence.

Like the other planets of the Solar System, the Earth probably formed from a cloud of dust and rocks whirling in space around the embryo Sun, some 4,600 million (4.6 billion) years ago. About 1,000 million years later, signs of life were appearing as microscopic organisms in the 'primeval soup' of the early oceans. However for more than 2,000 million years after these beginnings, life stayed very small and very simple.

Changing Earth
The earliest living things probably resembled the organisms called bacteria and cyanobacteria (blue-green algae) today. They are the simplest forms of life and make up a kingdom

Below: As the present day continents began to take form during the Jurassic Period, reptiles dominated all habitats, with dinosaurs ruling the land and crocodiles presiding over freshwater lakes and rivers.

Above: A well-preserved trilobite fossil (Calymene blumenbachii) *from Silurian times.*

of organisms known as the Prokaryota. It's believed that their activities helped to change the nature of early Earth. At first the atmosphere was rich in poisonous gases such as methane. However the biochemical activities of the first life-forms pumped increasing amounts of oxygen into the air. This was a source of ozone which began to shield the surface from the Sun's harmful ultra-violet rays (as it still does today). These changing conditions allowed the next steps in evolution – see Burgess Shales, pages 14-15.

Jelly to shells
From 2,000 million years ago, microorganisms grew in layered mounds of minerals in shallow water. These became well preserved as the objects known as stromatolites (shown in later pages of this book). Some stromatolites have been through the process of silicification, to form the kind of rock known as stromatolitic chert. Within these can be found amazingly preserved remains of the microbes. From about 1,000 to 800 million years ago there are increasing and tantalizing signs of multicellular organisms, perhaps resembling simple jellyfish: these might be called the first true 'animals'.

Fossils start to appear in appreciable numbers in rocks formed after about 540 million years ago. This was the

time that shelled creatures evolved in the seas. Shells, being hard and resistant to decay, fossilize fairly well. Living things before this time, from about 1,000 to 540 million years ago, had evolved greater size and complexity. But they were mostly jelly-like. Their soft bodies fragmented and rotted before preservation could occur. Only a few rare and precious fossils give glimpses into this misty phase of life's history.

From water to land
At first, life flourished only in the seas. Fossils form well in water, as organisms die and sink, and are

Origins of names
The names of the geological time spans called periods were mostly established in the 1800s. Some originate from the area where rocks of a particular age were first surveyed and studied. The Cambrian Period (540–500 million years ago) takes its name from Cambria, an old Roman-Latin term for Wales. Geologist Adam Sedgwick introduced the name in 1835 after describing rocks from North Wales. Other period names have their origins in the main types of rocks formed at the time. For example, the Cretaceous Period (135–65 million years ago) is so called from the huge thicknesses of chalk laid down as it progressed – *creta* ('kreta') is an old Latin term for 'chalk'.

Below: The ammonite Mantelliceras *is preserved in chalk typical of the Cretaceous Period.*

covered by silt, mud, sand and other sediments on the bottom. From the sea, plants moved into freshwater, and animals followed them. Their fossils show an increasing variety of forms. By 400 million years ago another major habitat was being conquered – the land. Until that time the ground had been barren, with no covering of soil as we recognize it. Pioneering plants and animals spread over the mud, sand and rocks, leaving their fossils as they colonized new areas. Their remains show that plants needed stiff stems to hold themselves up, since they were no longer buoyed by water. Animals could wriggle or squirm. But the more complex types changed their fins for limbs, and took their early steps over the ground.

Reptile domination

By 350 million years ago a new group of creatures had appeared, with scaly skin and waterproof-shelled eggs. These were the reptiles, and their fossils trace their climb to dominance.

Above: An early Palaeozoic plant, Moresnetia zalesskyii.

Below: Mesozoic brittlestars, Sinosura sp., from the late Jurassic Period.

By 200 million years ago they had given rise to the major large animals in all three major habitats – on land, as the dinosaurs; in the air, as the pterosaurs; and in the sea, as plesiosaurs and ichthyosaurs. Startling fossils of these great beasts, including their eggs and babies, and the animals and plants that shared their time, show how they lived and died.

Above: Early Cenozoic (Palaeocene) seedling Jaffrea speirsii, a relative of the living katsura tree in the magnolia group.

Below: Cenozoic mammoth hair dating from the Quaternary Period.

Above: The remains of a woolly mammoth and straight-tusked elephant being excavated from a clay pit in Sussex, England, in 1964. These large herbivores existed within the last 1.75 million years.

Towards the end of the 'Age of Reptiles', plants underwent a revolution. Conifers, ginkgos and similar trees had dominated for much of the era. But by 100 million years ago a new group, the angiosperms, were becoming established. These include the dominant plants we see around us today – flowers, herbs and broad-leaved bushes and trees.

Mass deaths

About 65 million years ago there was a great change in the types and varieties of living things. Dinosaurs, pterosaurs, plesiosaurs and many other groups of animals, and many plants too, all abruptly disappear. This is known as a mass extinction. It marked the end of the great time span known as the Mesozoic Era, 'Middle Life'. This era had begun with an even greater loss of life 250 million years ago, which had in turn marked the end of the previous era, the Palaeozoic or 'Ancient Life'. Following the Mesozoic came our own era, the Cenozoic or Cainozoic, 'Recent Life'. Each of these huge phases of life is documented by the types of fossils in the rocks, and the make-up of the rocks themselves.

THE GEOLOGICAL TIME SCALE

Fossils are records of life in the past. But when, exactly – how many thousands or millions of years ago? Palaeontologists and other scientists use a dating system known as geological time to put the various time spans of the past into perspective.

Rocks and the fossils they contain are dated in various ways, to find out how old they are in millions of years. These dates are fitted into a framework known as the geological time system. Its divisions are based on significant changes in the rocks and the types of fossils within them, as various kinds of life came and went throughout evolutionary history.

Eras and periods

As described on the previous page, the major divisions of geological time are termed eras. First is the Precambrian, when living things were mostly specks, although larger and more complex creatures resembling jellyfish and worms appeared towards the end. The Precambrian was followed by the Palaeozoic, Mesozoic and Cenozoic Eras – Ancient, Middle and Recent Life respectively. In turn, each of these great eras is divided into spans called periods. Most of these periods lasted a few tens of millions of years. Again, the transition from one to the next is marked by important changes in fossils, as extinctions of previously dominant organisms occur and new types take over.

Epochs

As we progress from the past towards the present, the amounts of fossils, and their details of preservation, generally increase – because earth movements, erosion and other forces have had less time to destroy them. Also, the technologies used for finding the age of a rock or fossil are more accurate with younger specimens. This allows increasing accuracy of dating in the Cenozoic Era. So the next-to-last and current periods, the Tertiary and Quaternary, are subdivided into shorter time spans known as epochs. Further subdivisions do exist, but are often used to date rocks on a more local scale.

Useful shorthand

The names of the eras, periods and epochs act as 'shorthand labels' to enable palaeontologists to define and communicate a fossil's place in the past.

Precambrian Era
4,600–540 million years ago

Palaeozoic Era
540–250 million years ago
• Cambrian Period
540–500 million years ago
• Ordovician Period
500–435 million years ago
• Silurian Period
435–410 million years ago
• Devonian Period
410–355 million years ago
• Carboniferous Period
355–295 million years ago
• Permian Period
295–250 million years ago

Mesozoic Era
250–65 million years ago

• Triassic Period
250–203 million years ago
• Jurassic Period
203–135 million years ago
• Cretaceous Period
135–65 million years ago

Cenozoic Era
• Tertiary Period
65–1.75 million years ago
  • Palaeocene Epoch
  65–53 million years ago
  • Eocene Epoch
  53–33 million years ago
  • Oligocene Epoch
  33–23 million years ago
  • Miocene Epoch
  23–5.3 million years ago
  • Pliocene Epoch
  5.3–1.75 million years ago
• Quaternary Period
1.75 million years ago – present
  • Pleistocene Epoch
  1.75–0.01 million years ago
  • Holocene Epoch
  0.01 million years ago (10,000 years ago) – present

Variations in dating

There are several variants of the geological time scale, used in different fields such as basic palaeontology, mainstream geology, geological surveying, and prospecting for fossil fuels. For example, in some systems the Cambrian Period starts 570, 560 or 543 million years ago, and the Jurassic Period begins 144 million years ago.

Also, in the US the Carboniferous Period is sometimes known by two other names, the Mississippian Period or System followed by the Pennsylvanian, with the split at about 320 million years ago. However the sequences of the names for the eras, periods and epochs remain the same in all of these time scales.

Right: Exposed rock in the Ouachita Mts, Missouri. The mountains formed in what US geologists would term the Pennsylvanian.

Palaeogene and Neogene

In recent years, some amendments have been suggested to the traditional dating system outlined above. These affect the Tertiary Period (65–1.75 million years ago) and its various epochs, which together account for almost all of the Cenozoic Era. Traditionally, the Tertiary was followed by the Quaternary Period – the tail-end of the Cenozoic – which ran to the present day. In the revised system, the Cenozoic Era is divided into two more equal time spans, the Palaeogene and Neogene Periods. The former takes in the Palaeocene to Oligocene Epochs, which remain unchanged. The Neogene includes the Miocene and later epochs to the present, which again remain unaltered. So in the scheme depicted below, the Palaeogene Period would run from 65 to 23 million years ago, and the Neogene from 23 million years ago to the present. Thus the familiar labels 'Tertiary' and 'Quaternary' are superseded. However, many areas of palaeontology move rather slowly, and numerous exhibitions, museums and collections still exhibit Tertiary specimens. For this reason, we have added 'Tertiary' and 'Quaternary' to the chart below, as they remain a point of reference for fossil enthusiasts.

Further amendments also affect the boundaries between recent time spans, such as shifting the end of the Eocene Epoch and start of the Oligocene from 33 to 34 million years ago, and likewise the end of the Pliocene Epoch and start of the Pleistocene from 1.75 to 1.8 million years ago.

Recording geological time

This chart shows one system of dividing the Earth's past into eras, periods and smaller time spans. The names are extremely useful shorthand for palaeontologists, geologists and others, as they do not always have to specify the numbers of millions of years ago.

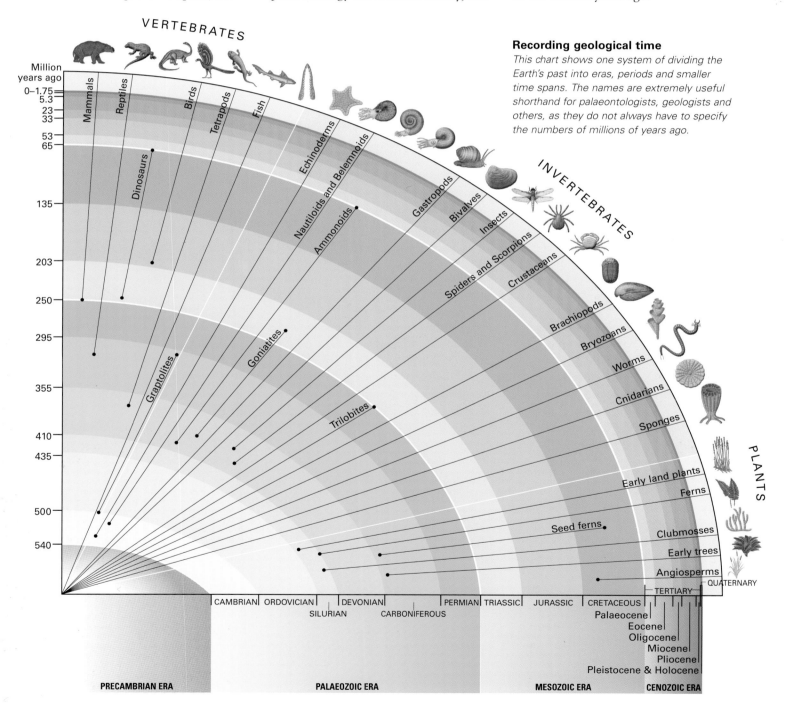

MAJOR FOSSIL SITES – THE AMERICAS

Some of the greatest fossil discoveries have been in the 'Badlands' of the North American Midwest – especially Alberta (Canada), and Montana, Wyoming, Colorado and Utah (USA). This is typical fossil-hunting country with bare rocks swept of soil by winds and rain, so that remains are easily spotted.

The landscape of the Badlands is subject to hot sun in summer, and freezing rain in winter, meaning plenty of erosion in the rocks as they weather, crack, peel and split, and fragments tumble down steep slopes or are washed away by flash floods. This ongoing geological activity continually exposes new layers with fresh fossils.

An embarrassing error

Perhaps the biggest 'fossil gold-rush' occurred in the Badlands region towards the end of the 19th century. It involved dinosaurs, of course, as well as many other reptiles, and plenty of other creatures, plus plants too. It was partly a result of bitter rivalry between two eminent palaeontologists, Edward Drinker Cope and Othniel Charles Marsh, and their respective teams of prospectors, workmen, restorers and benefactors. Their conflict began in about 1870, as an early wave of 'dinosaur-mania' was sweeping North America. Cope invited Marsh to view the remains of a long-necked, tubby-bodied, four-flippered, sea-going reptile, a plesiosaur called *Elasmosaurus*. Marsh noticed that Cope's reconstruction had the skull on the tail rather than the neck! From this time the two men were locked in competition to find the best fossils.

Below: Excavating dinosaur fossils on the Patagonian plains.

The first fossil gold rush

The intense antagonism of Cope and Marsh continued until their deaths in the late 1890s. Between them they named about 130 new kinds of dinosaurs and well over 1,000 other animals, from sharks to mammoths. Some of these finds have not stood the test of time, due to the race, rush and confusion of the so-called 'Bone Wars'. However the energy of the two men enthused many fellow fossil-hunters, and today North America vies with Asia (mainly China) to have the most fossil plants and animals described and catalogued.

The Burgess Shales

In 1909 eminent American palaeontologist Charles Walcott explored a quarry high in the Rocky Mountains near the town of Field, British Columbia. He came upon an astonishing treasure trove of fossils now know by the general name of 'the Burgess Shales'. The remains dated back to the Cambrian Period, some 530 million years ago. Walcott was astounded at the detailed state of preservation, which had occurred so fast that it entombed not only hard-shelled animals but also soft-bodied creatures like worms before they had time to rot away.

The Cambrian explosion

However, Walcott was less able to accept the incredible diversity of living things at such an early time – worms, sponges, jellyfish, arthropods related to crabs, and many more. According to beliefs of the time, creatures from that long ago should not be so diverse or varied. Life should have had started small and simple, and gradually worked up to the complexity and variety we see today. This idea is embodied in the concept of the 'evolutionary tree of life'. The tree

Above: A fossilized bee, more than 35 million years old, found in Colorado, USA.

began, long ago, with a trunk and a few branches, then expanded and diversified to the myriad twig ends of the present time. But finds such as the Burgess Shales show that this was not the case. Rather than a tree, an unkempt hedge might be a more apt comparison, with many branches appearing here and there throughout evolutionary time, some dying out rapidly but others enduring for much longer. The Burgess Shales represent one of these early bursts of evolution, which included the first shelled creatures. The time is often called the 'Cambrian explosion'.

South America

The number of significant fossil finds in South America has increased considerably since the 1960s. In particular, this continent lays claim to possibly the earliest, one of the biggest meat-eating, and the biggest of all dinosaurs – *Eoraptor*, *Giganotosaurus* and *Argentinosaurus*. Many other fascinating finds have come to light, often as a result of modern mining operations – in particular in Bolivia. Specimens include insects, frogs, small mammals and other creatures from the Tertiary Period, encased in amber.

Right: Map of the Americas, showing some of the major fossil discovery sites.

1. Colville River, Alaska, USA
2. Red Deer River, Alberta, Canada
3. Burgess Shales, Field, British Columbia, Canada
4. Hagerman Fossil Beds National Monument, Idaho, USA
5. Dinosaur National Monument, Utah/Colorado, USA
6. Como Bluff, Wyoming, USA
7. Kansas Inland Seas, USA
8. Joggins, Nova Scotia, Canada
9. Rancho La Brea, Los Angeles, USA
10. Texas Red Beds, USA
11. Santana Formations, Araripe Basin, north-east Brazil
12. La Paz Oligocene beds, Bolivia
13. Valley of the Moon, Ischigualasto Park, Argentina
14. Cerro Condor and Chubut, Argentina

MAJOR FOSSIL SITES – EUROPE, AFRICA

Collecting and displaying fossils as objects of beauty and intrigue – 'nature's sculptures' – gained popularity in Europe in the 1700s. So fossil-rich sites became well known even before people appreciated that these items were the remains of once-living things.

One of the first people known to make a living from fossil-hunting was a young woman, Mary Anning (1799–1847). Mary lived and worked in Lyme Regis, Dorset, South West England. Here, the coast is continually being eroded as waves eat into the cliffs. The region is sometimes referred to as the Jurassic Coast; many of its rocks were formed on the sea bed during this period, as countless marine creatures died and sank and were subsequently buried. The curly patterns of preserved ammonite shells are especially plentiful. Mary was one of those people who easily developed a 'good eye' for the best fossils, spotting tell-tale signs that enabled her to quickly distinguish fossilized creatures from ordinary rocks.

Fossil fame
Mary Anning spent her days on the Lyme Regis foreshore with her geological hammer and basket, gathering impressive specimens which were sold to private collectors and museums. She has a remarkable record of finds, including one of the first ichthyosaurs (dolphin-shaped sea reptiles) to be unearthed, in 1814; a virtually complete plesiosaur

Below: The 'Jurassic coast' of Dorset, UK.

(tubby-bodied, long-necked sea reptile) in 1824; and probably the first discovery in Britain of a flying 'pterodactyl' or pterosaur, in 1828. The shorelines near Lyme Regis still throng with fossil-hunters today.

Exquisite quality
Some of the world's most well known and valuable fossils come from the Solnhofen quarries of Bavaria, Germany. The limestone here is very fine-grained, known as 'lithographic' limestone since it was formerly quarried for use in printing. The seven or so preserved specimens of the first known bird, *Archaeopteryx*, were discovered in the area. So were the fossils of one of the smallest dinosaurs, *Compsognathus*. The amazing detail and quality of preservation allows study of their minutest features, including the feather structures of *Archaeopteryx*. These suggest that this bird, rather than being a clumsy glider, could truly fly – although probably not as aerobatically as most birds today.

The Karoo
Great Karoo Basin, centred around Victoria West in south-central South Africa, houses one of the largest and most important sets of fossil deposits in the world. Most of the rocks date

Above: After World War I, a team of scientists from the British Museum travelled to Tendaguru, Tanzania, to study and remove dinosaur fossils, including Brachiosaurus. *The main excavations had been done by German palaeontologists prior to this.*

from 270 to 230 million years ago – Permian to Early Triassic Periods. The rocks are divided into layers or series, which are (from oldest to youngest) the Dwyka, Ecca, Beaufort and Stormberg series. Long ago the climate was much damper than today. Ancient reptiles, in particular, roamed the luxuriant shrublands and swamps, and included mammal-like reptiles, pareiasaurs, titanosuchids and the smaller gorgonopsians.

Cradle of humankind
The vast continent of Africa is still relatively unexplored by fossil experts, but many palaeontologists accept that humans evolved here. Fossil remains of several kinds of prehistoric humans have been recorded. They range from smallish ape-like types who walked almost upright some five million years ago, to the first of our own kind, *Homo sapiens sapiens* or anatomically modern people, beginning around 150,000 years ago. Some experts recognize five or six main kinds of ancient human in Africa, while others contend there were twice as many.

Right: Map of Europe and Africa, showing some of the major fossil discovery sites.

1. Elgin, Scotland
2. Isle of Wight, England
3. Bernissart, Belgium
4. Neander Valley, Germany
5. Messel Quarries, Germany
6. Solnhofen, Bavaria, Germany
7. Beziers, France
8. Teruel, Spain
9. Tenere, Niger
10. Hadar, Ethiopia
11. Lake Turkana (Rudolf), Kenya
12. Olduvai Gorge, Tanzania
13. Tendaguru, Tanzania
14. Mafetang, Lesotho
15. Karoo Basin, South Africa

MAJOR FOSSIL SITES – ASIA, AUSTRALASIA

The tropical zones of the world, especially southern and South-east Asia, tend to be covered with lush vegetation and so have yielded few fossils. However, arid regions such as the Gobi and Australian deserts, with their exposed, eroded landscapes, are much more productive.

The vast arid stretches of Mongolia's Gobi Desert were first explored for fossils in the 1920s. Expeditions organized by the American Museum of Natural History visited the area, in the quest for the 'missing link' between apes and humans. One of the group's leaders was Roy Chapman Andrews, a larger-than-life taxidermist-turned-adventurer who always wore a ranger hat and carried a gun. The expedition sent back regular reports of exciting, perilous encounters with bandits and sandstorms – rather different from the usual staid world of palaeontology. Andrews is often identified, having been transplanted from palaeontology to archaeology, as the inspiration for the fictional movie hero Indiana Jones.

Remarkable finds

The Gobi rocks explored by the American expedition were far too old for human remains. Some dated to the Oligocene Epoch, 30–25 million years ago. Others were even more ancient, having formed in the late Cretaceous Period, some 70 million years ago, towards the end of the Age of Dinosaurs. However the expedition did

Below: Dinosaur egg fossil discovered in Mongolia – the first such egg to be found.

Above: Cambrian sponge fossil found in Archaeocyathid limestone, South Australia.

score some tremendous finds. One was the first known nest of dinosaur eggs, associated with the pig-sized, plant-eating horned dinosaur *Protoceratops*. One of the richest fossil sites in the Gobi became known as the Flaming Cliffs and continues to reveal major finds. Another exceptional find at Hsanda Gol was the remains of what is still the largest known mammal to have dwelt on land, *Paraceratherium* (formerly called *Indricotherium* and *Baluchitherium*). This vast Oligocene beast stood almost five metres tall at the shoulder and weighed 20 tonnes.

Scales and feathers

Some of the most astonishing fossil finds in recent years are from China's north-eastern province of Liaoning. Many are from the Early to Middle Cretaceous Period, 130 to 90 million years ago. They include some of the strangest dinosaurs ever found, and an incredible diversity of birds. Many of these creatures were covered in feathers, including some of the dinosaurs. The small predatory dinosaur *Microraptor gui* had feathers on all four limbs – the only known animal to exhibit such a feature. Exceptional preservation conditions in fine-grained rocks have helped to reveal the secrets of how and why feathers evolved.

More surprises

In addition, Liaoning has yielded fossils of mammals larger than any others dating from the Cretaceous Period. It was long believed that no mammal from the Mesozoic Era, the Age of Dinosaurs, was much larger than a rat. *Repenomamus gigantus* was dog-sized, resembled a small bear, and weighed in at about 15 kilograms, thereby overturning the accepted idea. Fossils of its cousin, the possum-sized *Repenomamus robustus*, reveal the remains of a small young dinosaur called a psittacosaur inside its body region – presumably its last supper.

Ediacara

In 1946–47 Australian geologist Reg Sprigg was surveying the Flinders Range of mountains in South Australia, seeking new deposits of the valuable metal ore, uranium. In the Ediacara Hills, Sprigg began to dig up strange fossils, the like of which had never been seen before. They dated back to Precambrian times, some 575–560 million years ago. They were soft-bodied life-forms, so unlike anything else in the fossil record, or alive today, that it's still not clear if some are plants or animals. Only a chance event meant they were buried rapidly and preserved swiftly, and then survived more than half a billion years to the present. These organisms, from a time before limbs or shells or fins, are now known by the general name of Vendian life. In contrast, the Riversleigh Quarries of Queensland have only been studied since the 1980s. They contain one of the world's densest concentrations of fossils, from the Late Tertiary Period, including kangaroos and marsupial predators resembling big cats.

Right: Map of Asia and Australasia, showing some of the major fossil discovery sites.

1. Hsanda Gol (Shand Gol),
   Mongolia
2. Nemegt Basin, Mongolia
3. Beipiao, Liaoning, China
4. Chaoyang, Liaoning, China
5. Umrer, India
6. Lufeng, China
7. Guangxi, China
8. Riversleigh Quarries, QLD,
   Australia
9. Muttaburra, QLD, Australia
10. Roma, QLD, Australia
11. Ediacara Hills, SA, Australia
12. Lightning Ridge, NSW, Australia
13. Dinosaur Cove, VIC, Australia
14. Mangahouanga, New Zealand

WHAT BECOMES A FOSSIL?

In theory, almost anything that was once alive could become a fossil – even a scrap of the jelly-like tissue from the soft body of a sea creature. In practice, most fossils are formed from hard parts of animals and plants, such as teeth, bones and shells, or tree bark and cones.

There are a number of popular misconceptions about what makes a fossil. Some people automatically think of dinosaurs, and ignore everything else. At the other end of the spectrum, the term 'fossil' once referred to any natural mineral object like a stone, rock or pebble. Today the accepted definition of a fossil involves an organic origin – an object that was once living. This includes all organisms or life-forms and parts thereof, from microbial organisms, tiny plants and

Above: The formidable killing claw of Dromaeosaurus albertensis *was carried on the second toe of each foot.*

Above: A Tyrannosaurus *tooth dating from the Cretaceous Period, recovered near the Red Deer River, Alberta, Canada.*

Above: In modern terminology, all 'fossils' have originated from once living matter.

Below: The scales, fins and tail of this fish, Notaeus laticaudatus, *have been particularly well preserved in marl.*

insects such as ants and gnats, to the greatest trees, sharks, dinosaurs, whales and mammoths.

Disappeared without trace

When most living things perish, they begin to rot and decay. Their remains may be decomposed by fungi and bacteria, and torn up, burrowed into or crunched to pieces by all manner of scavengers, from maggots to hyaenas. What is left weathers into fragments by the action of sun, rain, wind, ice and other elements of weather. In the water similar decay occurs, aided by waves and water currents, and the decomposing actions of fungi, worms, bacteria and others. So the vast majority of living things die and disappear without trace. They are recycled by natural processes back into the ground, lake or river bottom, or sea bed. They leave no fossils.

The harder, the better

Fossilization usually takes a long, long time, and is a chance-ridden process. As a result, usually only the harder parts of living things are preserved as fossils. These are the parts that resist decay, rot and scavenging, and which persist long enough for preservation to begin. Again, popular myth says that only bones form fossils, and perhaps teeth too. But there is a long list of other parts which are prime candidates for fossilization, as follows.

Plant parts

• The ribs or veins of plant leaves. (These are sometimes seen in winter, when the fleshy areas of the leaf have disintegrated to leave a 'skeleton' of harder, woodier veins.)
• The bark and wood of trees and other tall plants with trunk-like main stems.
• Roots, which are often among the hardest parts of a plant, and are usually underground, away from rotters and scavengers.
• Plant seeds, many of which are designed to resist harsh conditions such as winter, and then spring to life as they germinate when their surroundings improve.
• The woody cones of trees such as firs, pines and spruces.
• The thin, stiff, needle-like leaves of these various conifer trees.
• Pollen grains, which are tiny but tough, and resistant to most physical damage. Many are microscopic but

Above: The fossilized shells of bivalves.

they are produced in countless quantities, which improves the chances that some will be preserved.

Animal parts

• Shells or hard body cases, especially of molluscs such as snails and in the past, ammonoids and nautiloids. This includes the outer body casings or exoskeletons of insects, although these are usually only thick and resistant enough in certain examples, such as the hardened wing-cases, known as elytra, of beetles.

Spines

This very variable category of parts that might fossilize includes any long, narrow, sharp body projections. Spines occur on creatures as distantly related as sea urchins, spiny sharks (ancient fish), hedgehogs and porcupines. Often they fall from the main body after death and are preserved singly or in jumbled heaps.

Below: Whereas the spines of smaller creatures such as sea urchins may be relatively small, others – such as the ancient spiny shark Ctenacanthus *– boasted pretty sizeable protrusions. The specimen below is a preserved spine (or ray) from one of* Ctenacanthus's *enormous fins, and it measures some 19cm (7.6in) across.*

• Bones. Only the vertebrate or backboned animals possess true bones, which make up a skeleton. But then, not all vertebrates have bones – a shark's skeleton is made of cartilage or gristle, which is softer, bendier and more likely than bone to disintegrate.
• Scales, especially of fish and certain types of reptiles. In particular the large, hardened, bony scales, known as scutes, which covered certain dinosaurs, crocodiles, and fish such as sturgeons, are usually good candidates for fossilization.
• Teeth. These are possessed by most vertebrates, and certain other creatures like sea urchins also have tooth-like structures. For instance, in some snail-like molluscs the tongue is known as the radula and has hundreds of micro-teeth for scraping and rasping food. At the other end of the size range, the tusks of mammoths and other elephants were giant overgrown teeth.
• Horns. Usually these have a bony inner core covered with the hard, tough but light substance which itself is called horn (or keratin – see below). Various prehistoric mammals such as antelopes, cattle and rhinos had horns. There were also horned dinosaurs, or ceratopsians, such as *Triceratops*.
• Antlers, which are possessed chiefly by male deer and which are different from horns. They are formed of skin-covered bone and are shed each year to regrow the next, unlike horns, which are generally permanent and grow through life.

Above: Unearthing the remains of a 40 million-year-old giant whale, now in the desert at the Wadi Hitan 'Whale Valley' reserve, 150km/ nearly 100 miles south-west of Cairo, Egypt.

• Claws, nails and hooves, which are all formed from the same horny material as horns, known as keratin. Cats and birds of prey have sharp claws, the hoofed mammals or ungulates possess hoof-tipped toes, and most monkeys and apes have flattened nails similar to our own.

Above: The veins of a leaf Delesserites *from the Palaeocene Epoch.*

Below: Fossilized animal bones in a cave.

HOW FOSSILS FORM

Fossilization is a very variable process. It depends not only on the physical nature and chemical composition of the parts being preserved, but also on the nature of the sediments which bury them, water content, temperature, pressure, mineral availability and many other factors.

Fossils form in several ways. The 'normal' method is described here, and variations are included over the following pages, according to different habitats and conditions. The standard process occurs when a whole organism – or more often, parts of it – are buried. This usually happens in the sea, when a dead animal sinks to the bottom. It is covered by mud, silt or other small bits known as sedimentary particles. These are washed along by water currents or float down from above as the fine 'rain' of tiny fragments that settles continuously on the ocean floor. In general, the faster this initial burial, the better the state of preservation will be, since the animal or plant has less time subjected to decay, scavenging and disintegration.

Sediments and minerals

More sediments build up on top of the buried parts. This increases the thickness of the layers and the depth to which the parts are covered, and so increases the pressure on them. Gradually the pressure and squeezing begin to force together the particles, compressing the sediments harder and harder. Gradually, too, water seeps or percolates through these sediments, carrying with it natural minerals. These minerals slowly replace the organic substances or materials in the buried parts. The ongoing process of mineral replacement is known as permineralization.

Turned to stone

The original parts may be squashed, distorted and shattered during this phase, in which case the fossils are destroyed. In other cases the parts

Above: Soft-bodied, brittle-shelled creatures such as trilobites are often found fossilized in a squashed shape. These, of the genus Angelina, were recovered from the Late Cambrian Tremadoc Beds of Merioneths, Wales.

retain their original size and shape, and even their detailed inner organization, as their organic molecules and microstructures are replaced, one by one, by the inorganic minerals of rock. If the process continues to completion, then the original parts become completely

Below: How a fossil forms, stage by stage.

Stage 1: A hard part of a once-living thing, here symbolized by a single animal bone, resists weathering, scavenging and decay.

Stage 2: The part is washed into a river and sedimentary particles such as sand, mud or silt slowly settle and cover it.

Stage 3: Over time, more sedimentary layers collect on top. The part and its layer are squashed by the increasing weight.

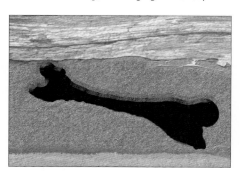

Stage 4: Minerals in the original part are dissolved and washed away, leaving an empty space or hollow chamber – a mould.

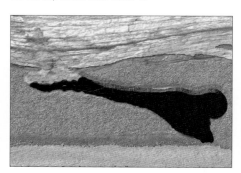

Stage 5: The space is filled by further minerals which trickle or percolate in from the surrounding rocks, forming a cast.

Stage 6: Earth movements, erosion and other processes gradually remove the upper layers, so that the fossil is eventually exposed.

Above: Rock strata are beautiful exposed in the iconic, partially eroded sedimentary landscape of western North America's canyons. The geology of these canyons is rich in the fossilized remnants of plant life and vertebrate animals.

inorganic or rocky. This is called petrification and is summarized in the handy but limited phrase 'bone to stone'. Meanwhile the rock around has been buried and compressed, and its grains and particles are cemented together by natural minerals too. As a result, the original parts of the plant or animal have become rock encased in rock.

Rocks that contain fossils

Because of the way fossils form, they are found only in certain types of rocks, known as the sedimentary group because they began as layers of sedimentary particles. Sedimentary rocks include sandstones, limestones, siltstones, mudstones and shales. In addition to sedimentary rocks, there are two other major groups of rocks: igneous and metamorphic. Igneous rocks form when original rocky material melts under great pressure and temperature and then cools again. Molten lava that flows from volcanoes hardens into igneous rock. The original rocky material may be sedimentary rock containing fossils, but melting in

the igneous phase destroys them. Likewise, metamorphic rocks form when original rocky material is transformed by tremendous pressure, heat and chemical changes, but without actually melting. Again, if the original material had fossils, these are usually destroyed during the metamorphosis. The practical result of all this means that it's no use looking for fossils in igneous rocks, like basalts, granites or rhyolites, or in metamorphic rocks, like marbles, schists or gneisses. Usually, only sedimentary rocks will do, as shown on geological maps.

Moulds and casts

On occasion, as sedimentary rock forms around a piece of an animal or plant, the percolating mineral-laden water dissolves the part and washes it away. The result is a hole, space or chamber in the rock, of the same size and shape as the original part. This is a 'negative imprint' or impression, which paleontologists often refer to as a mould fossil. At a later time, this space may itself be filled by more minerals seeping in from the water and rock around. Now the result is a cast fossil, again of the same size and shape as the original organism part, but composed of a different selection of minerals and crystals.

Tiny part of a tiny part

It should be emphasized that at any time, in any of these processes, pressure and temperature and general earth movements can warp, twist, fragment and destroy fossils. Only a tiny proportion of plants and animals begin the preservation process. Only a tiny proportion of these end up as still-recognizable fossils. And only a tiny proportion of these fossils actually see the light of day, when we find them – the rest lie deep and undisturbed.

Trace fossils

Fossils which are not preserved actual parts of an animal or plant, but objects or signs made by them, or left by them, are known as trace fossils. Examples are footprints, burrows, nests, feeding marks and tail-drags. Perhaps some of the most unlikely are coprolites – fossilized droppings, lumps of dung and similar animal excreta. In their original state, coprolites would be squishy and smelly. But the preservation process turns them into hard objects made of rocky minerals.

Below: Fossilized fish coprolites originating from the Triassic Period.

FOSSILS IN THE SEA

Seas have covered most of the Earth's surface for most of its history. Sediments may be washed from land into the sea, where they settle on the bottom. The result is that the majority of fossils are from sea creatures, plus a few marine plants too.

It may seem strange that fossils found on high ground, such as the Burgess Shales in the Rocky Mountains, or the Vendian creatures of Australia's Ediacara Hills, came originally from life at the bottom of the sea. The answer lies in 'dynamic Earth' and its geology. The hard outer shell or crust of our planet is never still. Some of its activities are sudden and awesome, like a volcanic eruption, or an earthquake that sets off landslides, or an underwater earthquake that triggers tsumanis (giant fast-moving waves). But many other activities are too slow for us to see. Huge jagged sections or plates of the Earth's crust slide and drift, push into each other, or grind under or over their neighbours. Where plates collide, the rocks fold and buckle to build mountains. The forces of erosion such as sun, wind, rain and ice counteract by wearing away rocks. These changes may occur at the rate of just a few millimetres each year. But they have continued over the vast span of geological time.

Ancient seas on dry land

As a result rocks are continually on the move, forming and drifting, distorting and twisting, and being worn away or destroyed by the forces of erosion. This is how sediments that were once on the sea bed may be uplifted into mountains, and then eroded to expose their fossils. The layers or strata of sedimentary rocks always form horizontally, with level surfaces as particles settle under the force of gravity. But later earth movements can ripple and fold these rock layers like

Left: Parkinsonia ammonite recovered from Dorset, UK.

Below: A stunning example of fossiliferous limestone rich in the remains of ammonites.

Above: These 'chain coral' of the Silurian period (Halysites genus) are shaped like the links in a bicycle chain.

paper, and even twist and turn them upside down. Usually the youngest or most recently formed sedimentary rocks are nearer the surface, so that as we excavate down to deeper strata, we 'dig back in time'. Inverted layers can confusingly reverse this sequence.

The most fossils

As previously described, conditions for fossilization are most likely in the seas, because of the way sedimentary rocks form. Also, compared to land, seas and oceans have always covered much more of our planet. (Today, the proportion is about 71% for seas and oceans.) Both these factors mean that the vast majority of fossils are from sea creatures – especially hard-shelled ones. Indeed, some sedimentary rocks are almost entirely composed of fossils. They began as piles of dead shelly sea organisms. The fossil remains may be recognizable items or fragments of the organisms, such as the shells of limpets and sea-snails. These rocks are sometimes known as fossiliferous limestones. There are three main types:
• Biohermal limestones – formed by living things growing in situ, such as the tiny stony cup-like skeletons of corals, or accumulations of creatures anchored to the sea bed, such as crinoids (sea-lilies) or mussels.

Above: Shells are usually smashed by wave action, but in sheltered bays they are often more likely to be buried intact.

Right: Very muddy seashores may discourage scavengers, which also boosts the chances of marine life being preserved.

• Biostromal limestones – mainly shells and other fragments of dead animals washed about and generally piled up, such as brachiopods, trilobites, oysters and other bivalve molluscs, and sea-snails like whelks.

Ediacara mudslide

The amazing fossils of Ediacara, South Australia, are from soft-bodied organisms, which usually rot away far too quickly for preservation. Scientists have concluded that this Precambrian community must have been surprised by a sudden mudslide, perhaps triggered by an earth tremor. Suffocating mud covered the area so fast, and there was no escape for its inhabitants. The blanket of mud kept away scavengers, and the low-oxygen conditions within it prevented the action of bacteria and other microbes which normally cause soft-tissue decomposition.

Below: The puzzling fossil Mawsonites *was one of those recovered from the Ediacara Hills, northern Flinders range.*

• Pelagic limestones – mainly tiny floating life-forms whose individual shells are often too small to make out. These die in their billions and sink to the sea bed, forming the greater proportion of ocean-floor ooze, which gradually hardens into sedimentary rock. As a result, pelagic fossiliferous limestones usually have a smoother, fine-grained appearance compared to the lumpy texture of the other types.

Bigger sea creatures

Most fossils are bits and pieces of organisms. Rarely a plant or animal is preserved whole, with its parts still together, in the positions they were in life. For a vertebrate animal like a fish, this is known as an articulated specimen. Stunning articulated fossils of fish show us their exact size and shape when alive. Sometimes even the positions of their fins are visible. Even the remains of what they last ate may be preserved in the stomach and gut region. In general, the bigger the organism, the more likely it is to come apart during preservation. So complete articulated skeletons of sea reptiles like ichthyosaurs and plesiosaurs, perhaps metres in length, are truly exceptional finds. It's likely that the original animals died in calm waters and their carcasses settled quietly on the sea bed, to be covered quickly but gently by sediments.

Below: Whole specimens such as this spiny-finned fish Diplomystus dentatus, *recovered from Wyoming, USA, and dating to either the Palaeocene or Eocene Epochs, can tell us much about the habits of the creature. This lake species was a relative of the herrings, and its upturned mouth suggests that it fed on insects at the water's surface.*

FOSSILS IN SWAMPS

Swamps, marshes and bogs are good preservers. Their still waters are usually low in oxygen, which inhibits microscopic decay by organisms such as bacteria. Also, mud and quicksand are excellent traps for unwary animals, which are 'swallowed' whole by the mire, ripe for preservation.

At times in the Earth's history, more than half the world's land area was freshwater wetlands. Mosaics of swamps, marshes and bogs were interspersed with pools, creeks and islands of drier land, constantly changing their pattern and shape as water levels fluctuated with the seasons and passing centuries. Perhaps the best known time for such conditions was the Carboniferous Period, 355 to 295 million years ago. The climate was also much warmer then. Tropical floodplains were home to vast forests of lush vegetation, where huge insects dwelt, and giant amphibians lurked in the steamy dark pools.

Dominant plants

There were no broad-leaved trees in Carboniferous times, as there are in tropical jungles today. The dominant Carboniferous plants were huge clubmosses and horsetails. Both of these groups still survive, but now they are much smaller in size and numbers. The enormous Carboniferous clubmoss *Lepidodendron* grew to 40m/130ft – as

Above: Coal being mined in China. This rapidly industrializing nation depends on fossilized carboniferous plants for much of its energy.

tall as the typical modern rainforest tree. Fossils of *Lepidodendron* are common worldwide and often show the characteristic 'scaly' bark with its kite- or diamond-shaped old leaf attachments. One of the largest horsetails was *Calamites*, at 15 and sometimes 20m/50–65ft tall, also with a woody strengthened stem. Its fossils are found mainly in Europe and North America.

Above: One of numerous fern impressions recovered from the Late Carboniferous Coal Measures, Illinois, USA.

Below: The 'coal swamps' formed during the Carboniferous supported giant insects and early tetrapods (four-legged vertebrates).

Above: Swamps remain productive habitats today. Since Mesozoic times, alligators have been among their most dominant carnivores – as here, in the Cypress National Reserve, USA.

The coal forests

These vast green swamps of clubmosses, horsetails, ferns, seedferns, and the newer groups of coniferous trees and cycads, produced vast amounts of vegetative growth during the Carboniferous. As the plants lived and died, their remains toppled and sank into the shallow bogs and marshes. Decomposition was slow, since warm water is low in oxygen, and the organisms of decay soon used up what was left of the oxygen for their life processes. So the slow-rotting plant matter piled up thickly, and was compressed under the weight of more layers above. Today's results of these 'Carboniferous coal forests' are various forms of coal and similar fossils fuels. They took tens of millions of years to form. We mine them with eye-blinking speed. When we burn these fuels, we are actually releasing the Sun's light energy, which those plants trapped more than 300 million years ago.

Giants of the swamps

Lumps of coal sometimes split open to reveal patterns of leaves such as ferns and clubmosses, and occasionally, animal remains. These were from creatures trapped in the semi-rotting vegetation and turned to fossils. The Carboniferous swamps were home to the biggest flying insect ever, the dragonfly *Meganeura*, with a tip-to-tip wingspan of 70cm/28in. It was probably snapped up occasionally by a new and enlarging group of four-legged, land-dwelling 'amphibians' such as temnospondyls and anthracosaurs. The fossils of these are also numerous in some regions. A well-known temnospondyl was *Eryops* of North America. At 2m/7ft long, it was one of the early large predators, resembling a huge and fierce salamander. Also in the Carboniferous, the first reptiles appeared as small, slim creatures outwardly resembling modern lizards.

Very special fossils

In rare cases, the fleshy body parts or soft tissues of a living thing are preserved as carbon-film fossils. The organic molecules of the ex-living tissue decay very slowly in an unusual way, into a thin dark film of carbon-rich substances. The resulting fossils themselves may look like a smear of oil or a scrape of soot in the rock – and that is approximately what they are. Carbon-film preservation can show the outlines of whole soft-bodied creatures, and the shapes of tentacles, flaps and fins around harder fossilized parts of animals such as fish, amphibians and reptiles.

*Below: A carbon film impression of a Redwood tree leaf (*Sequoia*), from the natural history archives of Humboldt State University, California, USA.*

Slow decay

The same processes that occurred most abundantly during the Carboniferous Period have happened in other times and places, and continue today. The Jurassic Period, in the middle of the Mesozoic Era, also saw a warm, damp climate and luxuriant plant growth, which fed the enormous dinosaurs of the time. Their legacy is some of the largest single fossils ever produced – huge limb bones and vertebrae (backbones) bigger than a person.

After the mass extinction at the end of the Cretaceous Period, 65 million years ago, the first phase of the Tertiary Period – the Palaeocene Epoch – was another span of moist and temperate conditions. This may have been one factor in the burst of evolution which saw new kinds of mammals and tall, flightless, predatory birds rise to prominence on land, in place of the once-ruling dinosaur-like reptiles.

Left: A Lyrocephaliscus euri *frog skull recovered from Spitsbergen, in the Arctic Circle – a land once part of the tropics and rich in swamp life and lush vegetation.*

FOSSILS IN FRESHWATER

Rivers and lakes support a variety of freshwater and semiaquatic life, ranging from fish to snails, worms, amphibians and reptiles. Yet they are also magnets for thirsty land animals. Heavy rain and floods wash remains from the land into these bodies of water, making preservation more likely.

It's a quiet day in the prehistoric world. Creatures have come down the steep riverbank to drink, bathe and cool down in the placid waters. Suddenly the river surges – a flash flood from torrential rains upstream crashes around the bend and sweeps all before it. The fitter, more agile animals can leap up the steep bank to safety. The young, old, sick and infirm have no chance, and the rushing torrent soon carries away their struggling bodies. Hours later, when the main flood has eased, the carcasses lap onto a sandbank downstream. Scavengers gather and the rot sets. A few days later, another flash flood covers the partly bared bones with sandy sediments. The process of preservation begins – and we dig up the resulting fossils millions of years later.

The science of taphonomy
It's exciting to speculate how ancient animals and plants met their ends, especially when large groups of remains are all preserved together. This applies through all eras and periods of geological time. Land animals need to drink, and so pools and rivers have always acted as magnets for wildlife. How did a herd of prehistoric mammoths or a flock of ancient birds all end up in the same place, entombed together? The science of taphonomy delves into the gap between death and rediscovery. It examines the processes by which dead organisms become fossilized, and how the circumstances, surroundings and other chance events all contribute to the groups or assemblages of fossils which we eventually uncover.

Above: Stegoceras *dinosaur vertebra of the Pale Beds, Alberta, Canada.*

Below: Freshwater habitats have supported animal life for millions of years. In some freshwater habitats, the remains of creatures were preserved in the base rock beneath the substratum, or lake bed.

Above: An amalgamation of pond snail fossils (Paludina) preserved in rock.

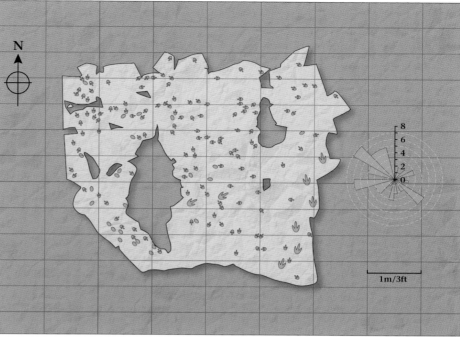

Prints on the bank

Footprints or paw tracks have created some of the most valuable trace fossils. They often occurred after animals had walked along riverbanks or lakesides, or across floodplains. The creatures made impressions with their feet, paws, hooves, claws, nails, tails and other parts, in the damp, soft clay, silt or mud. The indents were then dried and baked hard in the hot Sun. As the rains returned, another flood brought further sediments which filled the indentations, and so the fossilization process could begin. Many trackways of larger animals, such as dinosaurs, mammal-like reptiles and mammals, have been uncovered. In an area near Winton in Queensland, Australia, some 130 dinosaurs have left more than 3,200 prints in one rocky slab as they moved swiftly across the territory.

• The spacing of the prints (stride length) can suggest walking and running speeds.
• Print depth related to the firmness of the underlying sand or mud, and speed of movement, give valuable clues to body weight.
• Prints of many animals of the same kind and size, jumbled but all facing the same way, indicate a loose herd or family group on the move.
• Prints of the same kind but different sizes usually show a mixed-age group, with youngsters and adults.

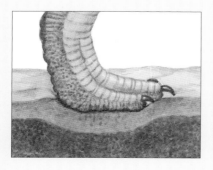

The matrix

Close examination of fossils and the rocky material in which they are encased, called the matrix, reveals many clues. If the surrounding particles of sediments in the matrix are all aligned in a similar direction, and the fossils are a dense amalgamation of remains from just one kind of animal or plant, this may be due to flash flooding and powerful currents which swept away and drowned a herd or group. More jumbled and randomly oriented particles, with a mixed assemblage of fossils from various animals, could indicate a slower, more gradual process of accumulation.

Freshwater life

In lakes and rivers, fossils usually formed as described previously, when remains were covered by sediments. There are fossils of freshwater fish, amphibians such as frogs and salamanders, and aquatic insects like diving beetles and dragonfly nymphs. As usual, hard-shelled creatures are among the most numerous fossils, such as pond snails and freshwater mussels. Apart from the details of the animal remains themselves, plant fossils preserved with them can help to distinguish between the freshwater of inland sites and the saltwater habitat of seas and oceans. Preserved stems of

Above: Plotting footprints onto a map offers a clearer perspective of the movements of the animal, and points towards behaviour – perhaps that it is seeking food or trying to escape from a predator.

reeds and rushes, leaf 'skeletons', and hard seeds and cones all indicate freshwater origin. Flat, lobed blades or laminae, and grasping finger-like holdfasts, are distinguishing features of seaweeds.

Below: Fossilized footprints often tell us whether animals travelled in groups, such as this herd of sauropod dinosaurs.

FOSSILS ON LAND

Most terrestrial (land-living) animals and plants which have left fossils were actually preserved in water – usually along the banks of rivers and lakes, or on seashores. Windblown sand or similar particles can also act as sediment to bury organisms in arid habitats.

Examples abound of creatures such as dinosaurs or prehistoric mammals being caught in a flash flood, drowned and buried under sediments on the river bed or lake bottom. Fossilization on dry land, without the role of water in any form, is rare by comparison. However, preservation may take place if the conditions are right.

Mummification

In very dry conditions, an animal carcass or dead plant may lose all its natural moisture and body fluids quite quickly, before decay can progress far. The micro-organisms and chemical processes that cause decomposition rely on the presence of moisture. So, once dried out, the remains may not disintegrate any further, or at least, do so very slowly. Plant scientists and florists use this technique for pressing flowers or making dried versions. This severe drying out of organisms is known as mummification.

Mummification can happen in deserts and drought-ridden conditions, and also in very dry caves. It's usually necessary for the remains to have some kind of physical protection against

Above: The dry, windswept, slowly-eroded Gobi Desert is a rich source of fossils dating especially from the Late Cretaceous Period, such as these dinosaur eggs.

wind, large swings in temperature, scavengers, moist air carrying microbes, and other agents which would cause them to degrade. This may happen when a dead animal is covered by sand in a desert storm, or is lost in a deep cave or tunnel.

A prelude to fossilization

Mummified remains of animals which became extinct relatively recently, like moas, mammoths, giant sloths and cave bears, are well known. However,

Above: The part-mummified flipper of a crabeater seal, preserved in the Dry Valleys of the Transantarctic Mountains, Antartica – a continent which is largely an 'ice desert'!

these specimens would not survive the rigours of geological time without further preservation. Mummification is usually seen as a helpful prelude to proper fossilization, with its entombment by sediments and mineral replacement. In such cases the initial drying out can help to preserve soft tissues such as skin and other features that would normally be lost. The giant tyrannosaur known as 'Sue' was partly mummified before true fossilization took place. So were some of the

Left: The remnants of plants, trees and even animal carcasses may be subject to limited decomposition, or 'mummification', in very dry or barren conditions.

Below: Petrified wood from a coniferous forest of Arizona, USA, from the Triassic Period.

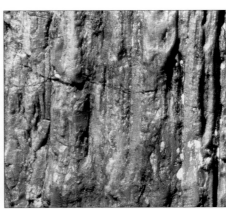

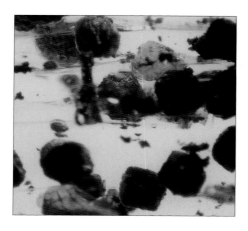

Above: Insect droppings preserved in Dominican amber, from the Late Miocene.

Trapped in tar

Here and there, natural deposits of tar or asphalt ooze to the surface and form pools. If these are covered by rain water, they may look just like waterholes, inviting animals to come and drink. But as soon as the thirsty creatures wade in, they become stuck and start to sink, gripped by the thick, gooey tar. Their struggles may attract predators, who try to approach – and they too are trapped. The animals sink and are preserved by the chemicals in the tar, often in great detail. One of the best-known sites for tar pit preservation is La Brea, in the suburbs of Los Angeles, USA. More than 600 species were preserved from 40,000 to 10,000 years ago, in a cluster of about 100 tar pits. They range from mammoths, mastodons, dire wolves, sabre-toothed cats, bison, giant sloths and short-faced bears to rabbits, rats, birds, lizards, insects and various plants.

Below: The Page Museum at La Brea holds an annual excavation of specimens, where visitors can observe professionals, and volunteers like the two people shown, recovering the bones of animals that drowned in the ancient tar pits here.

remains of dinosaurs such as *Protoceratops*, and their nests and eggs, which were preserved in the dry scrub of what is now the Gobi Desert, some 70 million years ago.

In the freezer

Another temporary mode of preservation is deep-freezing. Some of the best-known examples are mammoths, woolly rhinoceroses, giant deer and other large mammals trapped in the snow and ice of the far north – the tundra and permafrost across Northern Europe and Asia. Specimens are regularly exposed from the ice, especially by mining and exploration for gas, oil and mineral ore deposits across the vast wastes of Siberia. But as soon as the thaw sets in, so does decomposition. It's necessary to melt the remains very slowly and treat with chemical preservatives at once, in an ongoing process, to have any hope of stabilizing them over the long term.

Amber

This substance is the hardened, fossilized resin, gum or sap of ancient plants, especially conifer trees such as pines, firs and spruces. The trees make this resin partly as a form of sealant to cover any cracks, breaks, gashes or 'wounds' in their bark – just as our blood clots to seal a cut in the skin. Sometimes smaller creatures passing by, such as flies and other insects,

Above: 'Dima' the baby mammoth was found in permafrost on the banks of the Kolyma River, Siberia, in 1977. She was believed to be between 6–8 months old at the time of her death, some 40,000 years ago.

spiders, centipedes, even small frogs and lizards and mammals, become stuck in the adhesive, glutinous secretions. So do plant items like windblown pollen, seeds, petals and fragments of leaves or twigs. If the resin or sap continues to ooze fairly rapidly, it may cover and encase the specimen, preserving every tiny detail. Amber contains some of the most beautiful and spectacular of all fossils, giving valuable insight into the evolution of small and delicate creatures that are hardly ever preserved in the usual way. A few specimens of amber date as far back as the Early Cretaceous, but most are from the Tertiary Period. Famous deposits occur in the Dominican Republic, Caribbean and the Baltic region of Europe.

Below: Cold and frozen conditions drastically slow decay and allow time for preservation.

GREAT FOSSIL-HUNTERS

In 1770 Dutch chalk miners unearthed what looked like the huge skull, jaws and teeth of a weird and wonderful creature. It was nicknamed the 'Meuse monster', after the region in which it was discovered. The great find prompted a heated debate about the creature's origins, and captured the public's imagination.

Theories about the Meuse monster's origins prompted more and more speculation. Were there more 'Meuse monsters' still alive in the depths of the sea? Was the beast a victim of a biblical catastrophe? Was the find a fake, put there by pranksters – or even by the Almighty, in order to test people's religious faith?

Monsters and myths

The 'Meuse monster' fossil made headline news around Europe. All of a sudden, ordinary folk began to imagine an exciting long-gone world populated by huge beasts. The specimen was examined by Georges Cuvier (1769–1832), who acknowledged that its kind were probably long extinct, and who named it *Mosasaurus*. Cuvier was the most famous and respected biologist of the time. He began the work of studying, naming and classifying fossils according to the same principles used for living things – a novel and slightly heretical idea at the time. Cuvier was based at the Paris Museum of Natural History, which was then the biggest scientific organization of its kind in the world. His specimens included many fossil reptiles and mammals from the Tertiary rocks of the Paris Basin.

The country doctor

In the 1830s tales began to surface about more great beasts from long ago, which had left fossil remains such as teeth, jaws and bones. Gideon

Above: Dr Gideon Algernon Mantell was a country doctor as well as a palaeontologist. However, his greatest 'discovery', the teeth of the dinosaur Iguanodon (see below), was probably made by his wife, Mary Ann.

Mantell (1790–1852) was a doctor from Sussex, England. He consulted Cuvier about some teeth he had found, about 1820, which resembled the teeth of a living iguana lizard but which were much larger. Mantell was a keen collector of fossils, and travelled widely to examine and obtain specimens. He also had a home museum where he proudly displayed his best finds. In 1825 Mantell decided to call his new find *Iguanodon*, meaning 'iguana tooth'. He imagined it as a massive, sprawling, plant-eating lizard.

Above: British doctor Gideon Algernon Mantell named one of the first dinosaurs, Iguanodon. *Mantell's fossils consisted only of teeth, and it was more than 50 years before complete skeletons were found in Belgium. The creature is now believed to have been a four-footed herbivore.*

Above: Sir Richard Owen was responsible for the naming of the fossil group Dinosauria. He is pictured here holding the enormous leg bones of a moa, a flightless New Zealand bird that was ultimately hunted to extinction.

Fossils become fashion

In 1842, Richard Owen (1804–92) produced a report on fossils of great reptiles. Owen was an expert anatomist and would become Superintendent of the British Museum of Natural History – now the Natural History Museum, London. His report suggested that certain reptiles known from fossils should be included in a new group, the Dinosauria, 'terrible lizards'. Its members included Mantell's plant-eating *Iguanodon*, and also *Megalosaurus*. This was named in 1824 from a fossil jawbone with large sharp teeth, by William Buckland (1784–1856), Professor of Geology at Oxford University.

The general public became more interested in dinosaurs as giant fearsome beasts from long, long ago. Their fascination increased sharply when Owen joined forces with sculptor Waterhouse Hawkins to produce life-sized models of the great creatures.

Above: The French palaeontologist and anatomist Georges Cuvier did much to propagate the principles of functional comparative anatomy, and courted controversy by classifying fossils by criteria usually reserved for living things.

These were displayed in the gardens of the Crystal Palace exhibition centre in Sydenham, south-east London from about 1854. People travelled from all around to gather open-mouthed around the reconstructions. Dinosaurs hit the news and fossil-hunting became the latest fashionable pastime among gentlefolk of the period.

Below: The decision to mount life-sized dinosaur models at Crystal Palace, south-east London, was due in part to a surge of public interest in prehistoric creatures.

Fossils go west

During the mid-1800s 'fossil fever' spread to North America. In 1868, life-sized models of dinosaurs such as *Hadrosaurus* were displayed in New York's Central Park. By the 1870s Cope and Marsh (see Major Fossil Sites – The Americas) were racing to see who could recover the most fossils. In the wake of the hunt for dinosaur remains, many other kinds of fossils were also found, studied and named. Some of the greatest contributors to the breadth of information that resulted are as follows.

• **Richard Lydekker** (1849–1915) published a vast 10-volume catalogue of fossils at the British Museum of Natural History (now The Natural History Museum), in 1891. His book *A Manual of Palaeontology* (1889) was for many years the 'bible' of fossil collectors and restorers.

• **Barnum Brown** (1879–1968) was perhaps the greatest collector of fossils in the early 20th century. Working for the American Museum of Natural History, he led explorations to the Red Deer River region of Alberta, Canada from about 1910 to 1915, and further excavations at Howe Ranch, Wyoming in the 1930s. He is perhaps best remembered for finding the first *Tyrannosaurus rex* specimen in 1902.

• **Eugene Dubois** (1858–1940), a Dutch anatomist, shook the world when he

Above: Richard Lydekker's cataloguing of specimens for A Manual of Palaeontology, *published in the late 19th century, created an inspirational resource for fossil-hunters seeking a means of identifying and categorizing their finds.*

announced his discovery of 'missing link' fossils in Trinil, Java, in 1891. He named the remains as 'upright ape man' *Pithecanthropus erectus*. Today these fossils are included in the profile of the species *Homo erectus*.

The Sternbergs

As families of fossil enthusiasts go, there are few to match the Sternbergs of North America. They were father Charles H (1850–1943) and sons George, Charles M and Levi Sternberg. As well as actively collecting specimens, they assisted both the science and hobby by devising many on-site fossil-hunting techniques, such as encasing fragile specimens in protective jackets or casts, as well as ways of copying fossils using latex rubber.

Below: Charles Sternberg Senior reflects on some of his collected fossils. He was one of the USA's most pioneering palaeontologists and fossil-hunters.

GREAT FOSSIL-HUNTERS (CONTINUED)

If the previous centuries saw the rise of palaeontology as a charismatic science, modern times have certainly kept the pace. During the 20th century, some staggering new finds reshaped many assumptions about the prehistoric world, and also marked a greater involvement for the amateur fossil sleuth.

During the 20th century, fossil-hunting and collecting spread around the world as a popular pastime for many and a profitable profession for a few. Some dipped into it as a hobby, while others retained a lifelong interest. And some known for contributions in other fields have also held a fascination for fossils.

Little-known fossil sleuth

Marie Stopes (1880–1958) is best known as a pioneer and writer on sex education and women's health issues. From 1921 she established Britain's first family planning or 'birth control' clinics. But in her early career Marie studied plants and fossils. In 1905 she became the youngest DSc (Doctor of Science) in Britain, and first female science lecturer at Manchester University. Marie studied cycads and other ancient plants and showed how their remains could decompose and fossilize to form coal.

Lucky find

Rarely, amateur fossil-hunters strike it lucky. Most of these instances involve dinosaurs. In 1983 William Walker was searching a clay pit, as he often

Below: Dr Marie Stopes, palaeontologist and later – more famously – social reformer.

did. A plumber and part-time quarry worker, at a pit in Surrey he noticed a claw-like fossil – a gigantic one that measured more than 30cm/ 12in. Local experts informed London's Natural History Museum, and staff soon determined that plenty more remains were at the site. The result was *Baryonyx walkeri*, 'Walker's heavy claw', a meat-eating dinosaur some 10m/33ft long. *Baryonyx* was a different kind of carnivore from others known at the time, and so of tremendous scientific value.

Time and experience

Ten years after Walker's discovery, another part-time palaeontologist entered the spotlight. Car mechanic Ruben Carolini was a fossil enthusiast who spent much of his spare time out in the field. While visiting the 'Valley of the Dinosaurs' in Neuquen province, Argentina, Carolini spotted some exciting-looking bones and called in the experts, led by Rodolfo Coria from Carmen Funes Museum. The result – another great meat-eating dinosaur – was named *Giganotosaurus carolinii*, or 'Carolini's giant southern reptile'. It quickly became regarded as one of the biggest terrestrial carnivores – larger even than *Tyrannosaurus rex*. However, a 2006 review of already-known *Spinosaurus* fossils from Africa deduced that this spinosaurid was the world's all-time biggest land predator.

Right: William Walker's story is cheering to all amateur fossil collectors. His famous Baryonyx claw, discovered in 1983, provided important information about the spinosaurids, which were huge predatory dinosaurs. Walker unearthed his 'lucky find' in a clay pit when he was not actively looking for fossils. A reconstruction of Baryonyx appears below.

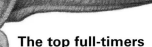

The top full-timers

At the other end of the scale to these chance finds by amateurs, are renowned professionals who regularly turn up breathtaking discoveries. Most work for museums, universities or similar institutions. They have teams of surveyors, diggers and other staff, and resources to plan, equip and finance excavations in great detail. Among the leading professionals of the past few decades are Paul Sereno (1957–) and Dong Zhiming (1937–). Sereno is attached to the University of Chicago and has made discoveries of immense importance in North America, South America and Africa. They included record-breaking dinosaurs such as *Eoraptor* and *Herrerasaurus*, which were among the earliest of the dinosaur group.

China's 'Mr Fossil-finder'

Chinese palaeontologist Dong Zhiming has led expeditions to many sites, including Yunnan Province and the Gobi Desert. He and his teams have unearthed, studied and named hundreds of new species, not only dinosaurs but mammals and other creatures. One of his prize finds was a quarry near Dashanpu, in Sichuan

Above: Chicago-based palaeontologist Paul Sereno, who identified a new species of dinosaur from bones collected in India, displays a model of the assembled skull of the 67-million-year-old carnivorous predator at an exhibition in Bombay. Working with Indian students, Sereno pieced together bones collected over a 20-year period from the western and central regions of the country.

Below: Giganotosaurus carolinii has been regarded as the largest known carnivore to roam the earth – a plaudit since taken by Spinosaurus. Amateur collector Ruben Carolini discovered the fossilized bones of this mighty meat-eater in Patagonia, Argentina in 1993, and a subsequent excavation unearthed a skull that was larger than any existing Tyrannosaurus. The reconstructed skeleton of this theropod is about 70% complete. Parts of a larger specimen have since been found, and indicate it was 8–10% greater in size.

(Szechwan) Province. This 'dinosaur graveyard' and has yielded thousands of fossils. At the museum on the site visitors can see large areas of fossils still partly embedded in the rocks.

Apart from dinosaurs, finds of early human fossils, and their relatives and ancestors called hominids, often grab the public's imagination (see also Famous Fossils, later in this section). Louis Leakey (1903–1972) and wife Mary Leakey (1913–1996) did much to establish East Africa as a centre for hominid evolution. In 1964 Louis and associates proposed the name *Homo habilis* ('handy person') for remains found associated with simple stone tools at Olduvai Gorge, Tanzania, from 1960. Mary and her team came upon the famous Laetoli hominid footprints in Tanzania, in 1978. The prints are dated to 3.7 million years ago and show a hominid with a true bipedal gait.

WHO OWNS FOSSILS?

Rules and regulations covering fossil-hunting are often quite vague – and, in any case, vary greatly around the world. This is rarely of consequence if people hunt fossils for pleasure, for their own personal collections and displays, cause minimal damage on site, and make no monetary gain.

Occasionally, there are problems when an unexpected find turns out to be very valuable or scientifically important. For example, assume a marvellous fossil is discovered, which is potentially worth a small fortune. Who gets the recognition and/or the money? In most cases, the actual finder, whether professional or amateur fossil sleuth, receives the recognition. Photographs of the specimen in situ with the person who spotted it are invaluable evidence in this respect, to ensure that credit is given where due. But the actual ownership of the fossil, and any profit arising from it, could be claimed by several parties, singly or in combination. They include:

• The landowner. This may be a private individual, a national or state organization like a heritage trust, or a business or commercial outfit such as a mining company.

• The benefactor or financier who has put up the funds to support the dig and pay for equipment, expenses and other costs.

Below: Fossil experts who lead walks and digs can advise on safety and legality, as can the local museum or palaeontological society.

• The leader, organizer or site manager of the dig, who takes ultimately responsibility for decisions about which fossils are worth excavating.

• The organization or institution which has set up and probably funded the excavation, such as a university, museum or palaeontological society.

• A commercial company which buys and sells fossils, and which may not be involved in a direct or practical way, but which has 'bought the rights' to any or all specimens yielded by the field trip.

Famous fossil battle

For day-to-day finds, such a list may seem fanciful. But there were months of discussions over who owned, and so had the right sell at auction, the enormous *Tyrannosaurus* 'Sue', worth US $8 million. This incredible specimen, the largest and most complete *T. rex* fossil ever discovered, was found in 1990 by dedicated fossil hunter Sue Hendrickson. A volunteer with the Black Hills Institute of Geological Research, South Dakota, Hendrickson was one of a party digging for fossils on land owned by

Above: Although educational trips to fossil sites are generally encouraged, schools should be careful to seek permission and ensure pupils are properly supervised.

Sioux leader Maurice Williams. Peter Larson, president of the Black Hills Institute, bought the rights to excavate the tyrannosaur for a comparatively small sum, but the validity of this sale was later contested by the US Federal Government. While her ownership was under question, 'Sue' spent time in transit under conditions that many palaeontologists argued would have a detrimental effect upon her bones. She was eventually sold in New York by Sotheby's, for the famous seven-figure sum, in October 1997, seven years after her discovery.

Public access

Some fossil sites have open access and can be enjoyed by virtually anyone at any time. The main examples are coasts and shorelines. Specimens can usually be picked up and removed without problems. On areas of 'common land' it may be possible to pick up a loose specimen lying at the surface. But any use of hammers or other tools, to chip and release an embedded fossil, is not advised. It could be viewed as illegal damage to the site, and legal claims of trespass and criminal damage could be brought.

For almost anywhere else, it is wise to obtain written permission from the landowner (see Collector's Code and

Transporting Fossils). This may vary from a quarrying company or private estate owner to a highways authority or district council. The local palaeontology or geology society can help with this, or it may require a visit to the local council or Land Registry office. It is one of many reasons why novice fossil-collectors are urged to join a local club or society.

Many owners of fossil-rich sites have standard agreements ready to sign, date and exchange. Part of the agreement is to absolve the landowner from any risk, and make the fossil-hunter solely responsible for accidents and injuries. Fossil sites may well be steep and rocky, with loose stones – and claims for injury compensation are an all-too-familiar part of modern life, so do observe the general Countryside Code at all times when out and about.

Fossil-rustling

Taking a fossil from a site or collection without proper permission is, in effect, stealing. The recent explosion in prices paid for the best fossil specimens has meant that cases of 'fossil-rustling' have tripled in the past 20 years. One of the most infamous is the so-called Maxberg torso specimen of *Archaeopteryx*, one of only seven or so fossils of this earliest known bird. The only specimen to be held as part of a private collection (in Pappenheim, Germany), the Maxberg mysteriously disappeared following the death of its owner Eduard Opitsch in 1991. Despite police investigations it has not been found and is now believed to have been privately sold.

Below: Other Archaeopteryx *fossils form part of collections in Germany, and at The Natural History Museum, London (shown).*

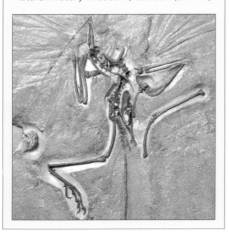

Special cases

Many valuable fossil sites, and other areas of natural beauty and special interest, have been made into national parks, wildlife refuges or heritage reserves. It is usually against the regulations to take any fossils or other items from these places. Some ill-informed amateurs may believe that a small fossil slipped into the pocket could not be traced. But an expert would soon analyze the specimen, its mineral make-up and matrix, and so pinpoint its place of origin.

Above: The gigantic Tyrannosaurus rex *fossil known as 'Sue' is now housed at the Chicago Field Museum, USA. The Museum famously won the bid for the bones, paying US $8.4m – the largest sum ever exchanged for a fossil, making 'Sue' a record breaker in every sense. 'Sue' is not a Jurassic specimen as many assume: rather, she is believed to have died at the end of the Cretaceous Period, possibly the victim of another tyrannosaur aggressor. Her discovery has greatly influenced the way in which palaeontologists perceive the movement and behaviour of these beasts. The fossils of 'Sue' were the subject of a protracted legal ownership battle between the landowner, the expedition sponsors, and the leading fossil-diggers.*

Countryside Code

In addition to various fossil-collecting codes, as detailed on the following pages, everyone is encouraged to observe the general rules of the Countryside Code when accessing rural land, whatever the reasons for doing so. In 2004, following new legislation concerning countryside access and the public's 'right to roam', the code for England and Wales was revised and updated. The rules focus on personal safety and the protection of the land.
• Be safe - plan ahead and follow any signs.
• Leave gates and property as you find them.
• Protect plants and animals, and take all litter away with you.
• Keep dogs under close control.
• Consider other people.
In addition:
• Beware of fire risks.
• Avoid damaging crops or disturbing animals.
• Respect the work of the countryside.

WHERE TO LOOK FOR FOSSILS

It sounds a little obvious, but the best place to look when starting to collect fossils is indeed a map. More precisely, several maps, especially geological maps showing rock types and ages, as well as guidebooks, and perhaps a visit to the local museum, fossil shop or antiquities centre.

The usual countryside map is a helpful starter, showing roads, towns, railways, parks, simple topography and similar features. This is useful for planning the trip and accessing the site. A geological map is also needed. This is available for purchase from specialist map suppliers, or perhaps for loan or hire from a local club or society. Geological maps show the general types and ages of rocks present or outcropping at the surface, as areas of lines and colours. Experts also employ satellite images and remote sensing to locate and survey new sites.

The right rocks

As described earlier, fossils are nearly always found in sedimentary rocks. So regions of igneous or metamorphic rocks are of little interest to fossil hunters. The age of sedimentary rocks is also important. If you have become

Above: It is important to take great care when gathering fossils from locations that could present hazards to the collector, such as unstable cliff edges. As a precaution, safety helmets (hard hats) should always be worn.

Below: The first geological map of Great Britain, drawn by William Smith (1769–1839). Many of his topographical studies were centred around the spa town of Bath in England, where he lived for much of his life.

interested in, say, fossil mammals, then it's little use targeting rocks from the Palaeozoic Era. Likewise if you are looking to build a collection of trilobites or ammonites, then Tertiary rocks are too recent and will not contain them.

Also, the names of rock and mineral types can be bewildering to anyone unfamiliar with them. So it's advisable to read the maps in conjunction with a good rock-and-mineral guide book or identifier. In addition, a general guide book for the locality should describe areas of public access, private land,

Fossil-collector's Quarry Code

- One individual or party leader should obtain prior permission to visit a quarry or mine.
- Visitors should be familiar with the current state of the quarry, and consult the manager for areas which have access or hazards.
- Arrival and departure must be reported to the quarry office on every visit.
- Safety hats are usually compulsory; stout boots are also essential.
- Visitors should keep away from vehicles and machinery.
- All blast signals and warning procedures must be understood.
- Quarry faces and rockpiles are highly dangerous and liable to collapse without warning – stay away.
- Beware of wet sand and lagoons of spoil or sludge.

(See also the general Collector's Code in this section.)

Right: Forbes Quarry was the site of Gibraltar's first Neanderthal human find, in 1848. Five sites for Neanderthal finds have now been identified on 'The Rock'.

Inland cliffs and bluffs

Outcrops of bare rock occur in many drier regions of scrub and desert. Hot days and cold nights alternate to expand and cool the rock, so that it cracks and flakes. Winds may pick up sand or dust and blast the exposed surfaces. Also the winds and occasional flash floods wash away particles to prevent soil formation that would cover the bare ground. So fresh fossils appear regularly at the surface.

River valleys

In some regions, rivers gradually cut their way downwards, exposing layers of rock as they go. Sometimes the layers or strata are clear enough to be 'read like a book', yielding different kinds of fossils from their various ages of formation. However eroded, rocky riverbanks can be steep and slippery, with difficult access.

nature reserves and national parks and similar. This helps to decide when permission may be needed.

Types of sites

In many places, surface rocks are covered up: by soil, trees, crops, roads, buildings, golf courses and many other features. Fossils are most easily identified where rocks are bare and preferably in a continual process of being freshly exposed. This can happen by natural processes such as weathering and erosion, or by a range of human activities. Such sites include:

Coasts and shores

Waves, winds, tides, undercut cliffs, rolling boulders and rockfalls mean that seashores and coastlines are some of the best of all fossil sites. A visit after a storm may reveal marvellous new exposures. However the very agents that erode the rocks can present great danger too. So extra care is needed, especially with an eye on the tides to ensure that you are not trapped or cut off.

Below: The cave of Jebel Qafzeh, Israel, has yielded the remains of several Homo sapiens *up to 100,000 years old.*

Quarries and mines

Some of the best fossil finds have come from mining and quarrying sites. Vast amounts of ores, minerals and rocks are worked, exposed and removed. However the site owners may have strict rules about fossil collecting, so that it does not interfere with the operation of what is an extremely expensive business (see panel).

Cuttings

Artificial 'valleys' cut for roads, railways, canals and even pipelines can present many fossil-hunting opportunities. However the land is owned by someone, and permission should be sought. The noise and activity of a busy road or railway line nearby not only presents hazards such as fast-moving vehicles, but can also be very tiring and distracting.

Caves

Fossil-hunting underground, in caves and tunnels, is a specialist activity that needs expert help. There are many dangers such as lack of light for working, seeping gases, and possible cave-ins or floods. Some professional excavations of caves have unearthed important ancient human remains.

PLANNING THE TRIP

Nearly every region has a geology or palaeontology society, natural history club, local museum and history group, rock-and-mineral association, or similar organization. Both careful consideration and expert advice will help to ensure that the trip does not become a wasted opportunity.

Regional and local groups undoubtedly offer enormous benefits to the keen but inexperienced fossil hunter. They can advise on planning and equipment, likely finds, and perhaps loan items of equipment such as tools and containers. There are also the benefits of shared experience and social interaction. A visit to the local museums also helps, to see the types of fossils found in the locality.

Another way of gaining experience is as a volunteer on an organized dig by a museum, university or similar institution. This can vary from a day or two at a local site, to a longer period in a more exotic location. Some holiday companies specialize in these types of breaks and vacations. It can be an invaluable experience to mix with the experts, and learn from their knowledge with 'on-the-job training'.

Equipment

Proper preparation and equipment make fossil-hunting infinitely more pleasurable and rewarding than when without these items. A collection of tools, bags and other kit can be built up over time. It need not be expensive

Below: The fossil collector's kit should contain items both for personal safety as well as for exposing specimens on site.

– ordinary household items or do-it-yourself tools will often do, until the proper versions are affordable.

Clothing and safety

Warm, comfortable clothes, that fit loosely and do not chafe, are a must. People today are much less accustomed to spending all day outdoors, with the sun – or rain – beating down. Several layers of shirts and jumpers, plus a hooded waterproof jacket or coat, are ideal. So are stout shoes or boots.

Above: With field gear safely tucked away in portable rucksacks, you are free to make and record observations about what you see.

Rocks are usually hard and sharp, so gloves are very important. A safety helmet or 'hard hat' is obligatory in some situations, and always helpful near tall rock faces. Sunglasses or a peaked cap help to shield the eyes from glare, especially from light-coloured shiny rocks. Goggles or a visor protect the eyes from flying shards of rock while hammering. And a mobile phone is an excellent aid in case of accident or injury.

Location and recording

Maps, local guide books, and fossil or mineral field identifiers are invaluable, usually in compact pocket form. A magnetic compass helps to locate the site in detail and orientate the finds, for example, the direction of fossilized footprints. A field notebook with pencil (and sharpener) or waterproof-ink pen is necessary for notes and sketched records. Modern lightweight cameras are a boon for 'point-and-shoot' photographs of fossils.

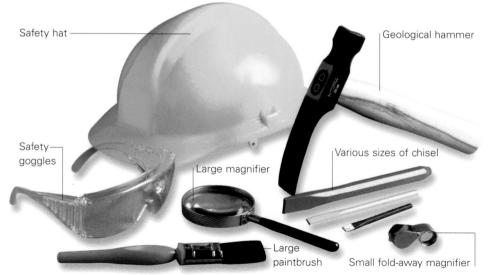

Safety hat

Safety goggles

Large magnifier

Geological hammer

Various sizes of chisel

Large paintbrush

Small fold-away magnifier

Felt marker pen

Clear plastic bags

Tweezers

Notebook for recording finds

Kitchen paper

Camera

Map

Selection of writing tools

Compass

Above: The above items are essential for recording the details of finds both in situ and partly removed, and should be present on site.

Field tools

The main hand tools for fieldwork are:
• Geological hammer, with one blunt face and one pick-end.

Construction sites

As builders and construction companies dig footings and foundations, they may expose fossil-containing rocks. However, they may not always welcome fossil hunters. Having extra people on site can cause problems with safety, insurance and the use of machinery. Also a large, urgent construction project is unlikely to pause while a few fossils are recovered. However, it's always worth asking …

Below: An informal chat with construction staff on site may quickly reveal whether or not the type of items being uncovered are likely to be of interest.

• Guarded chisels, usually 'cold chisels' with hardened blades and plastic hand grips which protect against hammer blows to the hand. (Wood chisels are not suitable.)
• A mallet for use with the chisels, although the geological hammer may suffice.
• Trowels, large and small, for lifting and picking at loose items.
• Brushes, generally a small and large paintbrush, for sweeping away fine loose debris. Shaving brushes are excellent.
• Hand lens or magnifier, to study small details.
• Sieves, to separate actual specimens from loose sediments such as fine gravel, sand or silt. These can be lightweight plastic, of rigid or collapsible foldaway design.

Containers

A selection of plastic or canvas bags is ideal for carrying fossils. Newspaper, tissues or kitchen paper can be used to protect them in transit. Smaller specimens are safest packed into lightweight, rigid, plastic lidded containers such as sandwich boxes. See also equipment for plastering or jacketing fossils.

All of this, and more, is best carried in a sturdy backpack or knapsack. This leaves both hands free, is comfortable to wear rather than hold, especially when supporting packages of heavy fossils, and is easier to balance when walking in rough country with uneven terrain underfoot.

Photography and sketching

Some fossil-hunters take a few quick snaps of their finds in situ, but are later disappointed at the lack of clarity in the images. The undulating, random surfaces of rocks, and their often varied colours, mean that it can be difficult to make out shapes and objects. It is advised to take some photographs from directly above, and others from much lower viewpoints and from several angles, so that features can be identified by comparing these images. Shadows can be troublesome if they are from harsh flash or a low sun, but equally, lack of shadows when the sun is overhead also results in lack of definition.

Below: Many local museums display fossils excavated from the surrounding region. Staff are often willing to advise on the origins of particular specimens, which can help in the planning of a field trip to the local area.

DIGGING UP FOSSILS

Before setting out on a day's fossil-hunting, remember to tell someone reliable about where you are going and when you expect to return, supplying the relevant map references where possible. Also check the weather forecast, and revise the plan if it looks bad – digging really does require dry weather.

Think about personal necessities and sustenance before the trip – take food as necessary, and plenty of fluids. Being out in the sun and wind all day is thirsty work. On arrival at the site, carry out a quick survey and decide which areas look best for excavation, by a few short 'test digs' or blows with the hammer. Remains may already be 'eroding out' in some places. Look for shapes and textures that suggest fossils, like smooth curves of bone ends or regular lines and striations on shells, which distinguish them from the surrounding rock. See also the Collector's Code, later in this section.

Big to small

When digging for fossils, there are several basic guidelines.

• Go easy and take care. A too-hard hammer blow could shatter a prize specimen. If time is short or the weather turns foul, you may simply have to leave the fossil where it is, partly excavated. It will still be there tomorrow or the day after.

• Work from big to little, tough to delicate. Use the larger tools to remove unwanted rock, then work more sensitively and in greater detail as the specimen is exposed.

Above: A pair of protective gloves, that still allow sufficient grip and manoeuvrability, is important when working in the field.

• Work with the rock rather than against it, using its natural splitting or bedding planes to your advantage.

• Remove a block containing the fossil, rather than the specimen itself. Leave detailed exposure and cleaning until later, back at the workroom, where it is more comfortable and proper equipment is at hand.

• Don't forget to wear safety equipment such as goggles and gloves.

• Record each stage of the excavation with a simple map, a few sketches or (if you have brought a camera) photographs, and plenty of notes. The latter should include map reference and the surrounding rock types.

Above: This conifer wood bored by Teredo bivalve (shipworm) is an Eocene specimen from the Isle of Sheppey. It is a good example of a specimen likely to be tough to extract from rock without losing much of the detail.

Initial stages

Large quantities of material covering a fossil, known as the overburden, may be loose gravel, sediments or rockfall. It can be removed with a spade or perhaps a pick-axe. (Professionals sometimes use road-drills, jack-hammers, construction diggers or even explosives, but these are beyond most part-timers.) Then hammer and chisels can be employed. Keep an eye on the rock fragments as they are removed. If the fossil is well embedded in matrix, try to assess its overall size and position, and work around this, leaving plenty of room for error. Try a trial few blows on a rock of the same type which does not contain a fossil, to see how the rock reacts and splits or shatters. Do not chip or scratch the fossil itself, which could spoil its appearance and considerably reduce its scientific value.

Later stages

As the fossil is uncovered, switch to gentler methods. A small trowel or dental pick can lever out detached

Left: At a communal site, be careful not to stray onto a neighbouring patch, or damage delicate fossils with boots or piles of debris.

Shall I, shan't I ...?

Faced by a jumble of rocks and fossils at a new site, one of the most vexing questions for the novice fossil hunter is: Which specimen shall I choose? In other words, which ones will be worth the time and effort to excavate? Or even: Is it a fossil or just a weirdly shaped rock? For beginners, the answer is usually quite simple: Choose almost any one, since it will be valuable practice that brings precious hands-on experience.

Also consider: Would I wish to spend time cleaning up this specimen for my collection and perhaps display? It's wise to spend some time giving the whole site a brief survey, rather than stopping at the first attractive fossil. There might be a better-preserved, more complete version just a few metres away.

Below: Use of a geological hammer and chisel will preserve the fossilized specimen while separating it from the rock (and it would be safer wearing gloves).

Above: When uncovering larger fossils, an excavator carefully works around the specimen to remove 'overburden' and detach it from the surrounding matrix.

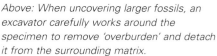

Left: Both a trowel and metal tray are useful items when sifting through sediment.

fragments. For very fragile fossils, a paintbrush, bradawl or dental-type pick may be suitable. It's best to chisel out a larger lump of rock around the fossil and lift out the whole item. Very fragile or crumbly specimens can be strengthened or stabilized as described later in the section.

Notes

Your notebook should contain plenty of jottings that record details such as locality, date, type of rock, position of fossil specimen, its size, notes on initial identification and other relevant information. All these details help to confirm formal identification later. A sketch can help to pinpoint an unusual feature, such as a spine or claw, that may not be easily visible on a photograph of the complete specimen.

Below: When labelling new specimens, for example by using corrective fluid and a ballpoint pen, be sure to mark the least important area, so that the fossil itself (like this small graptolite, to the right of the label) is not obscured.

COLLECTOR'S CODE AND FOSSILS

Each fossil presents a unique challenge for those tasked with removing it from the site and transporting it back to the workroom. Not least, some fossils are extremely heavy! As when digging up specimens, moving fossils could potentially disturb the local environment and should be conducted with great care.

Palaeontology and geology associations offer codes of behaviour when fossil-hunting. These are based on respect for the countryside and its inhabitants, as well as the need for caution and safety.

Field Collector's Code

1 Obey the Country Code and observe local byelaws. Remember to shut gates and leave no litter.
2 Always seek permission before entering onto private land.
3 Don't interfere with machinery.
4 Don't litter fields or roads with rock fragments that could injure animals or be a hazard to people or vehicles.
5 Avoid disturbing wildlife.
6 On coastal sections, check tides or local hazards such as unstable cliffs, if necessary with the Coastguard.
7 In mountains or remote areas, follow advice given to mountaineers and trekkers. In particular, inform someone of where you are going and when you are due back. Do not go alone.
8 Do not venture underground except with expert help.
9 Never take risks on cliffs or rock faces. Take care not to dislodge rock: others may be below.
10 Be considerate and do not leave hazards or dangers for those who come after you.

Below: Palaeontologists in Nigeria strengthen the weaker areas of a sauropod dinosaur bone before applying a hessian bandage.

Great weight

Most fossils are solid rock. So they are heavy. A hand-sized specimen is already a considerable weight to carry, especially when trekking on foot. A dinosaur leg bone may weigh several tonnes. So it's vital to be realistic about what can be transported back from a collecting trip. Much depends on whether vehicles can get near to the dig site. If not, it is best to budget for two or three trips on foot, from the site back to the car or truck, carrying sets of specimens each time. Although

Above: A palaeontologist examining a six million year old fossil in Abu Dhabi. The hot and arid conditions, and the sheer size of the fossil, make this a very challenging excavation.

you may be tempted to try and save time, if you try to carry lots of heavy specimens in one journey, you risk breaking them – or yourself.

Fragile fossils

Sometimes fossils start to crack or crumble as they are being excavated. The first response is: Is it worth continuing? Is the specimen valuable

Below: Further plaster is then applied to the bandaged specimen to complete the 'jacket' before the fossil is moved.

Below: Once the plaster has hardened the bone must be turned over so that the under surface can be fully encased within the 'jacket'.

Maps and grids

On larger sites, or when many fossils are preserved together, it's important to know their positions in relation to each other. This can help to reconstruct how the original organisms died and were preserved. Sometimes the site is covered by a grid of strings or wires, set at regular intervals such as one metre. Then the position and orientation of each fossil can be measured and plotted. This process continues with the excavation, so that the depth of specimens is also known in order to complete a three-dimensional location.

Below: This excavation of dinosaur bones in Nigeria illustrates how palaeontologists may be compelled to work within a tight, clearly-defined space, even when tackling the largest of creatures. The grid markers help the excavators to record the position of each part of the fossil.

Above: Excavation of a large dinosaur skeleton at Dinosaur Monument, Utah, Colorado, USA. As different sections of the specimen are uncovered, it is vital that the findings of each part are carefully recorded, to reconstruct accurately the creature's dimensions.

enough to warrant extra time and care? Perhaps there's another one nearby which is tougher and easier to remove. If not, then a weak or fragile specimen can be stabilized and protected in various ways, for example, by spray-on or brush-on adhesive or stabilizing compound, DIY spray-glue or purpose-made chemicals used by masonry restorers. This must be allowed to dry or set, so schedule time into the day to carry out other tasks during this period.

Jackets

Larger specimens that might crack or shatter can be protected and strengthened by jacketing. There are several common methods, usually involving plaster bandaging (plaster-of-Paris) or some type of glass-fibre resin or compound. One of the simplest ways is to use sheets of material or first aid bandages and ordinary plaster-of-Paris. An alternative is ready-made plaster-impregnated bandages as used to encase broken limbs, which simply need moistening. Wrap and smooth the jacket over the fossil and beyond, and allow plenty of time for it to set, before chipping the whole section free of the surroundings rock.

Wraps and containers

Each fossil should be put into a separate plastic bag – small transparent freezer-bags used for food are ideal. Tear off a piece of paper, write on the fossil's initial identification, as coded into your main notebook, and include this in the bag too. Smaller fossils can be put into rigid plastic boxes, but pad them to avoid rubbing and chipping. If there are no padding materials such as newspaper available, some dry vegetation like old leaves or grass stems will suffice.

Below: Uneven or largely-absent roads, and a shortage of road signs to indicate the direction of travel, are just two of the challenges that might confront a team of palaeontologists transporting fossils from remote locations.

CLEANING FOSSILS

Rarely, some fossils fall out of the rocks in almost perfect condition. All they need for display is buffing with a soft cloth, and a discreet label. But in most cases, specimens benefit from some judicious preparation and sympathetic cleaning.

Before rushing to clean and prepare a specimen, there are some questions to consider.

• Is it really worth a place in the displayed collection? What seemed like a fine example when you were removing it, out in the field some time ago, may not now seem quite so marvellous. It may have been eclipsed by specimens you found subsequently. On closer examination, it could have small flaws or chips. It might be very similar to a specimen you have already prepared or obtained. In these cases it might be worth saving for your general 'background' or reference collection, but without too much time spent on preparation since it will probably not go on display.

• How much should it be cleaned? Leaving some surrounding rock or matrix in place may add artistic merit and 'character' to a fossil. Take some time to look at real specimens in

Above: Some kind of magnification tool may be required in order to work out where the fossil ends and the matrix begins.

museums and exhibitions, and of photographs of specimens in books and on websites. See how sometimes only a portion has been exposed and cleaned up. The result can be more dramatic, as the fossil 'appears' mysteriously from its background, while at the same time providing enough scientific information for firm identification.

The work space

For cleaning and preparation, you need a clear working space with a hard non-slippery surface, such as wood, which does not matter if it chips or dents. Beware of fragments of rock flying away from the specimen as you work. Some preparators arrange series of long, low, upright panels around the work surface, like fencing, to stop this from happening.

Below: Items such as safety goggles and a face mask are a useful safeguard against dust thrown up when cleaning specimens. Before beginning to clean, wash your work space with a clean cloth or sponge, and keep a pair of protective gloves on hand, particularly if handling chemicals such as dilute acid.

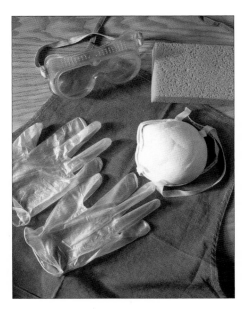

Always do a 'test run'

Whichever technique you use to clean a fossil, try it first on an unwanted fragment of rock, or on one of the less important specimens, or on a less important surface of the main specimen which will not be visible on display. If things go wrong, you have not lost your most prized example. Or at least, the problem will be 'round the back' when the item is displayed.

Below: Dilute acid is carefully applied to a disposable area to see if the specimen contains certain reactive minerals, some of which may help to dissolve the matrix.

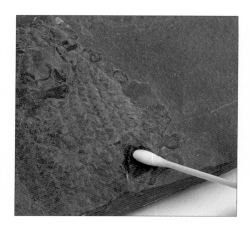

Above: For specimens without much adherent matrix, simple household items such as cotton buds (swabs) or small brushes can be useful when cleaning specimens. These can also be used to remove small patches of sediment once more rigorous methods have been tried.

Above: Similarly, a soft paintbrush can push away friable matrix in small amounts if used delicately – caution when applying strokes to the surface of the specimen is the main thing to remember. The brush can be washed and dried regularly to prevent clogging.

Above: A miniature sandblaster, powered by compressed air, helps to remove loose sediment without damaging the specimen.

Above: A vibrating pen, or 'vibrotool', is powered in a similar fashion, and can help to define the shape of a specimen.

Plenty of light from a couple of desk lamps, one on either side to minimize shadows, is important. Try not to place the light sources on the opposite side of the specimen from yourself, otherwise the areas you are working on will be shaded. Goggles for eye protection against flying shards are also strongly advised.

Experts usually clean smaller fossils while looking through a magnifier lens on a stand, or through a binocular (two-eye) microscope. This helps to protect your eyes and prevent eye strain as well as giving a closer view.

A fishing-tackle box or toolkit case, with small drawers and compartments, makes a good container for tools and equipment. Similar many-compartment cases intended for items such as screws and bolts, available from do-it-yourself

and hardware outlets, are very handy to store your specimens while they are being prepared.

It helps if you have a room or corner to leave this equipment laid out in place, rather than having to set it all out and then pack it away again after each session. If tools and specimens can be left out, covering them with a cloth or sheet will prevent dust gathering, which tends to dull the colour of fossils and obscure detail.

Cleaning with chemicals

Often a fossil is different in mineral composition from the matrix around it. If the fossil is much harder, it may be possible to brush away soft matrix, perhaps after softening or soaking it with water. You could test-soak unwanted pieces in water or perhaps

a dilute solution of vinegar, which may soften or dissolve calcium-rich matrix while leaving the fossil untouched. Fossils from the seashore may be soaked for a few hours in a watery, weak solution of bleach. This helps to remove the salt. Again, try these techniques on an unwanted piece first.

Another chemical method is acid etching. Kits of acid-etch equipment and solutions can be purchased from specialist fossil suppliers. This is a fairly complex, time-consuming technique and involves handling potentially harmful chemicals. Good ventilation is essential, and other safety precautions are also necessary. Sometimes local palaeontology club members band together to research, purchase and set up such equipment, so that it can be used during carefully monitored communal sessions.

Physical methods

When removing rock and matrix by physical means, it is advised to study the hidden shape and contours of the fossil, and where the matrix probably ends and the specimen begins. This can be done by consulting guide books and fossil identifiers. When chipping carefully with a lightweight hammer and narrow chisel, making sure the specimen is well supported so it cannot fly away or slide off the worktop. More delicate tools include awls, bradawls, dental picks and mounted needles for removing smaller and smaller particles. Even general household items such as cotton buds (swabs) and paintbrushes can be used.

Power tools

Powered engravers, drills or sanders can save much time. Dental drills and modelling power tools often have tiny circular-saw blades and fine file-like abraders for gradually and carefully removing adherent matrix. With all these methods, pause now and again to clear the dust. Take a wider view, from several angles, to check progress of the work. Power tools throw up a lot of dust and debris, so wear a face mask to filter the air, as well as the usual protective goggles.

IDENTIFYING AND STORING FOSSILS

After spending hours out in the field collecting fossils, and in the workroom cleaning them – what next?
Most collectors like to make a display to show off their prize specimens. But there is some forethought
and preparation to do first, such as setting the fossils in context.

Fossils can be admired for their simple shapes, colours and beauty. But this is like admiring a painting without the insight and knowledge of the painter, which period it dates from, the circumstances of the subject or scene, and how the work fits into the history of art. Likewise, identifying fossils and finding out which organisms left them – when and how and where – adds vastly to the interest and pleasure of owning and displaying them.

Identification

There are many ways to pin down the identity of a fossil. For some people a simple label such as 'ammonite' may suffice. But there are thousands of kinds of ammonites known from fossils, so it's worth delving more

Below: Identification guides, augmented by further information gleaned from the internet or museum displays, can help to pinpoint the origins of a fossil.

Above: Record as much information as possible about a specimen, though do keep to a consistent and acceptable labelling system for ease of reference.

Above: In addition to actually labelling the specimens, it is important to record corresponding information about your collection in a log book.

deeply into the science of taxonomy and the system of classifying living things. The traditional system starts with large groups, phyla, which are subdivided in turn into classes, orders, families, genera and species, as will be explained later. A name at the hierarchy level of family or genus is

usually sufficient for most amateur collectors, depending on the specimen's state of preservation and rarity. Identification is carried out by noting specific features, characteristics or traits in the specimen, as listed in classification keys, as well as by overall visual appearance, coupled with the age of the rocks and their general nature, such as sandstone or limestone, which indicates the original habitat of the organism.

Helpful aids to identification
• Pictures and notes in the later pages in this book.
• Similar pictures and lists of key features, in fossil guides and identification books.

Below: Specimens become dusty and details obscured if kept in open displays, so choose a suitable container for them.

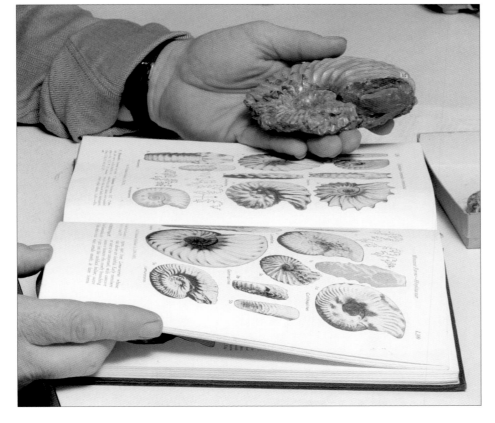

Left: Parts or fragments of one fossil item may be assembled like a jigsaw puzzle into the more complete version, simply by trial-and-error fitting.

• The same material from internet sites, which are a fast-growing resource for palaeontologists.
• Expert help and advice from knowledgeable people.
• Similar specimens in other collections, such as in museums or palaeontology societies.

Storage

Fossils that are not for display are best stored in rigid containers such as sets of drawers or compartments, which are dry and dark. Moisture and bright light can degrade several kinds of minerals. Purpose-made cupboards or chests of drawers, often with the classic shallow trays as used in museums, can be picked up at auctions, sales or house clearances. Or sets of wooden or plastic storage cases can be pressed into use. Open shelves are less useful, since dust accumulates and gradually dulls and obscures a fossil's detailed surface features. Remember that fossils are stone, and so heavy. Any storage system should be able to cope with the weight. The drawers, compartments or boxes should be clearly labelled with their contents, and arranged in some sort of logical order, for example, by time period or major groups of living things.

Below: Soft padding protects the fossils from scratches or cracks if the container is jolted. Do, however, avoid cotton wool or similar materials where fibres are likely to dislodge and cling to the specimen.

Labels, notes and indexing

Each fossil in a collection should be given a brief identification name and a unique code or log number. This keys into an index for the collection, which can be kept as cards in a box, in a loose-leaf folder or on computer disc. Information from the field notebook is transcribed onto a list for each specimen, along the lines of:
• Unique code, index or log number.
• Name, for example, to family, genus or even species level.
• Approximate date of preservation, from a period or era of geological time such as Carboniferous or Eocene, to much narrower or shorter units such

as ages or zones of time. This is linked to the type of rock in which the fossil was preserved, known as the lithological unit.
• Location and date of find, with map reference if possible.
• Nature of the matrix and features of surrounding rock.
• Special notes about the site, methods used for extraction or cleaning, glues and preservatives, and similar data.
• General information such as notes on palaeo-ecology (see next page), behaviour or lifestyle: 'active carnivore in shallow Silurian seas' or similar.
• To tie the fossil to its information, include a short label in its storage compartment. Or write the index code in indelible ink on an unimportant part of the fossil. Take fossils from their storage places one at a time, to avoid mixing and misplacing.

Below: Accessible museum displays may provide clues as to the identify of your fossils. Staff may allow you to handle them (always check), or the displays may be interactive, with information given at the touch of a button.

DISPLAYING FOSSILS

One of the greatest satisfactions of fossil-hunting is to build up a well-presented and informative display of the best specimens, so that other people can appreciate and understand these fascinating objects. This can be done by following a few very simple, practical tips.

Fossil displays can be a permanent installation, or 'collapsible' and brought out for special occasions. It's well worth putting some thought into what you would like to convey in showing a range of specimens together – the most interesting displays usually have some sort of linking theme or topic, for example:

• Varied fossils from the same locality at different times, illustrating the range of life which has populated the area through the ages.

• Fossils of the same geological age and site, revealing the variety of plants and creatures that lived together in the same place. This can allow reconstruction of a whole habitat and how the animals and plants lived together and interacted, an area of science known as palaeo-ecology.

• A group of organisms or similar fossils through time, such as sea-snails, petrified bark or fish teeth. These can be compared and contrasted to see how they evolved.

Below: Include notes on possible origins wherever you can. For example, it might be conjectured that the death of an entire shoal of fish (the species Gosiutichthys parvus, *shown below) was caused by poisonous gas in the water.*

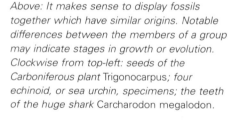

A practical display

Almost any size of display can be made attractive and informative, from a shoebox to a huge wall cabinet or stand-alone glass case. Ensure the case or container is presentable, perhaps with a coat of paint or paper lining that contrasts with the samples. Choose only the best specimens available – do not 'dilute' them with poorly preserved or broken examples. As your collection builds, you can transplant new and better finds to replace older, less impressive ones. Position and support each specimen at its best angle to show off the most informative side or face.

Above: It makes sense to display fossils together which have similar origins. Notable differences between the members of a group may indicate stages in growth or evolution. Clockwise from top-left: seeds of the Carboniferous plant Trigonocarpus; *four echinoid, or sea urchin, specimens; the teeth of the huge shark* Carcharodon megalodon.

You may need to trim off unwanted edges to make a pleasing shape and set the fossil to its best advantage. Include neatly printed labels or cards, both for individual specimens and groups of them. Or label a diagram or photograph of the collection as a key.

Selection

If you have a container or case for a collection, try various options of fossils before deciding on the final selection. Move them about and group them in different ways, to show similarities or contrasts. It's not unlike trying furniture in different places in a room, before deciding on the best layout.

*Left: The cut of the matrix around this attractive Late Cretaceous fossil (*Ctenothrissa radians*) is perfectly suited to an eyecatching stand-alone display.*

Sections and infills

Sometimes the broken surface of a fossil can be used to advantage. It may be sawn or cut off flat and then sanded and polished to reveal the inner structure of the specimen. This may be very beautiful, with colourful swirls or patterns of mineral crystals adding to the effect. Another option is to 'fill in' the missing part, to make the specimen whole again. This is usually done with some type of plaster or resin, but in a colour that contrasts with the actual fossil. The size, shape and contours of the infill can be gleaned from pictures of whole specimens. Attempts to blend the infill portion so that it looks like the rest of the fossil need great skill, and usually end up detracting from the overall effect. A faintly tinted clear plastic resin is another option for infills. It is usually better, more honest, and also scientifically acceptable, to make the infill very obvious.

Varnish or not?

Some collectors like to varnish their specimens. This may help to seal and stabilize the minerals. It may also deepen hues and bring out textures and colours. However over the long term, certain varnishes can degrade the minerals of the fossils. Also a shiny varnish means light glints and reflects off the surface, which can be irritating and obscure detail. However, some fossils are made by a process called pyritization. The original material of the organism is replaced by mineral iron pyrites. In moist air this is unstable and gradually disintegrates. Such fossils are best dried thoroughly and varnished to seal them from moisture in the air.

Below: Following expert guidance, museum staff may decide to add certain finishing touches to enhance or protect the surface of the reconstructed skeleton.

Above: Casts made of glass reinforced plastic are laid out prior to the mounting of the dinosaur Baryonyx *on exhibition panelling.*

Preserving

Sometimes a broken fossil can be mended with clear glue. As already advised, try the glue on an unwanted piece or surface first, to check it adheres and does not discolour. Fossils that are weak or crumbly can be stabilized with chemicals called consolidants, hardeners or protective resins, specially made for the purpose. Again, try them on unimportant areas first, in case they cause discoloration or a chemical reaction which may degrade the minerals.

Below: The tail of this Diplodocus *replica at the Natural History Museum, London, was temporarily replaced with a cardboard one while the original was being reconstructed.*

RECONSTRUCTING FROM FOSSILS

For certain people, finely preserved and well-displayed fossils, with a wealth of information about their origins, is not quite the end of the process. Some collectors like to take the next step, of trying to reconstruct or 'rebuild' an extinct plant or creature as it would appear in life.

Lifelike reconstructions range from sketches on paper, to illustrations 'borrowed' from books or websites for display, to simple scale models or even complex and detailed full-sized renderings. Most of the fossils in the later pages of this book have illustrations showing the appearance of the living plant or animal, as it looked millions of years ago. How do we know it is accurate?

Above: This atmospheric diorama combines life-sized model dinosaurs with: their habitat; the fossil skeletons used as the basis of the reconstructions; and an informative text panel with illustrations.

Below: Artists' reconstructions of prehistoric creatures, such as Pteranodon shown here, may show them feeding, fighting, breeding or in the company of similar species. Concurrent flora and fauna should also be depicted.

Above: Examining the surface of fossilized body parts, such as limbs, for scars and indentations made by muscle and other body tissues helps with reconstruction. Both of the above specimens originate from dinosaurs of the Cretaceous. Top is a toe bone of the plant-eating Maiasaura. Below it is a hoof bone of the big-horned Styracosaurus albertensis.

Composites

As we have seen, many fossils are just pieces or fragments of whole living things. Not only this – the parts can be squashed and twisted out of shape. One way around the problem is to assemble a composite version, using pieces from another specimen identified as the same species. There are many limitations on this method of 'borrowing' from some fossils to fill in missing sections of others. But the composite can help to give an general view of shape, size and features.

What colour were they in real life?

This question often plagues those making reconstructions of fossilized animals and plants. The short answer is – no one knows. A glance through a selection of fossil books will probably show the same famous creature, such as the earliest known bird *Archaeopteryx*, in a startling variety of plumages. Fossils are not original copies of the once-living matter. They are mineral replacement versions made of rock or stone. So they are the colour and pattern of their constituent minerals. Was a long-extinct fish or shellfish dull green or brown for camouflage, or brightly striped with pink and yellow to advertize its venomous sting or bite? Take your pick. When scientists, artists and modelmakers reconstruct extinct organisms, they have to make intelligent guesses as to the patterns and hues visible on the outside. Their informed guesswork is often based on the features exhibited by similar organisms, or living relatives.

Above: A safe option is to reconstruct an image of Archaeopteryx *using little colouring, or even in black and white.*

Above: A more adventurous rendering paints Archaeopteryx *in slate-blue shades. But even this might be a conservative treatment.*

Comparisons

There are also comparisons with living organisms. The science of comparative anatomy has a long and honourable tradition in palaeontology. For example, molluscs such as ammonoids no longer exist. But their modern cousins do, including the cephalopod mollusc group such as octopus, squid and especially the deep-sea, curly-shelled nautilus. Comparisons of ammonoid fossils with the equivalent parts of these living relatives helps to reconstruct the ammonoid's soft parts. Similar principles are used for all manner of ancient life, from simple plants to sharks, reptiles and whales.

A note of caution involves the process called convergent evolution. Organisms of different kinds come to resemble each other, generally or in specific features, since they are adapted to the same mode of life. A simple example involves the body shapes of certain fish like sharks, the extinct swimming reptiles known as ichthyosaurs, and modern dolphins. They have all evolved a similar streamlined body shape, with fins and tail, as a result of adaptation to speedy swimming, rather than because of any shared ancestry.

Flesh on bones

Some animals and plants are defined in size, shape and external appearance by their strong outer casing, such as a tree's bark or a trilobite's shell. This helps greatly to recreate their appearance in life. However most vertebrate animals – those with backbones – have an inner skeleton which may fossilize, covered with muscles and other soft tissues which hardly ever do. How are these fibres reconstructed by scientists?

Soft tissues can be built up stage by stage. Many fossil bones show roughened areas on their surfaces called muscle scars. These are patches where muscles were attached to the bones, and they may have flanges, ridges or crests on the bone to secure their fixings. Often they correspond to the muscle anchorage sites in modern relatives of the creature. The size and extent of a muscle scar indicates the size and power of the muscle which anchored there. So a fossil skeleton can be partly clothed in muscles. In turn, the musculature often defines the shape and contours of the whole animal, since muscles are generally clothed only by skin.

Right: A museum reconstruction of a chalk sea floor of the Cretaceous Period.

Below: A fossil of a sea floor at Kings Canyon, Northern Territory, Australia. The ripples in the rock were created by water movement.

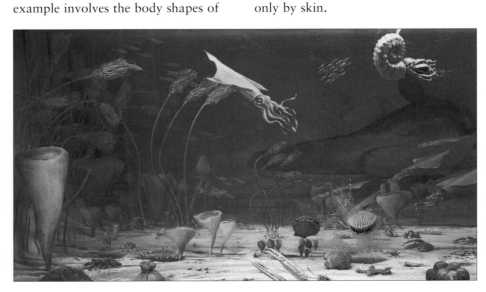

DATING FOSSILS

How old is a fossil? There are two main methods of dating or aging either the rocks themselves or their preserved remains, as used by geologists and palaeontologists. These are comparative or relative dating, and absolute or chronometric dating.

Palaeontologists often use comparative or relative dating, which deduces the age of a fossil by comparing it to the rock around it, especially the other fossils contained within this rock, and to the rocks and fossils in the layers above and below it. Because of the way sedimentary rocks form, the younger layers or strata usually overlie the older ones. So deeper fossil are older. Also the same sequence or series of sedimentary layers often crops up at many sites, with the same sequence of fossils within it. These sequences have been correlated and matched or combined to give an overall progression of rock types and fossils through the ages all around the world. This is known as general stratigraphic history. If a fossil comes from an isolated layer of rock, the features of this layer can be used to place it into the overall progression or stratigraphic history, and so the age is revealed.

Index fossils

Some types of organisms are very widespread as fossils, and they have also changed in a characteristic and

recognizable way through time. These evolutionary sequences are very useful for dating. The well-known fossils in them are known as index, marker or dating fossils. They help to pinpoint the time origin of more obscure fossils found with them. Common examples of index fossils include shelled marine animals, which formed plentiful remains in marine sediments and are often worldwide in distribution. (All are included on later pages in this book.) For instance:
• Trilobites are useful for dating Cambrian rocks.
• Graptolites are common and widespread index fossils for the Ordovician and Silurian Periods.
• Belemnites and ammonites show characteristic evolutionary sequences through the Jurassic and Cretaceous Periods.
• Foraminiferans, which are tiny and simple shelled organisms of the plankton, are used through the Tertiary Period.

Left: Successively aging rock strata are clearly visible in the steep walls of a canyon.

Above: A member of an excavation team from The Natural History Museum, London, uses a device known as a compass-clinometer. This measures the incline, or 'dip', of the bedding plane – the boundary separating one layer of rock from the layer above or below – at various magnetic compass orientations. Assessing the nature, formation and subsequent movement of each rock stratum will help the team to assess, from the position of the now-exposed fossil, its approximate age.

Absolute dating

Also known as chronometric dating, this method is based principally on the physical process called radioactive decay. Some minerals of the Earth's crust contain pure chemical elements that are radioactive (usually in a very minor, harmless way). Through time after their formation, these elements give off radiation energy (radioactivity), at a regular and constant rate. As they do so, they change from one form or isotope of a chemical element into another, or even from one element into another. Scientists can measure the relative proportions of different isotopes or elements in certain rocks, to deduce when the mineral formed.

Each isotope or element series has its own fixed rate of decay. Carbon is relatively fast, and is used in 'radio-carbon dating' for specimens up to about 70,000 years ago. Uranium decays very slowly and can date the oldest rocks, from billions of years ago. Potassium-argon decay is also widespread and commonly used for times spans greater than 100,000 years ago, mainly where there has been local volcanic activity and the rocks are rich in potassium. However, measuring radioactive decay involves complex and expensive scientific equipment such as mass spectrometers, which are beyond the finances of most amateurs!

In practice, absolute dating pinpoints the actual age in numbers of years, for a limited number of suitable rocks. There is usually a margin of error given. For example, rocks from the Cretaceous-Tertiary (Palaeogene) transition may be dated to 65.3 million years ago ± (+/- or plus-or-minus) 0.4 million years. The results from

Above: Samples containing fossil fungal spores being collected by scientists at Butterloch Canyon in Italy. The Permian-Triassic boundary between these rocks is visible as the dark sediment line running around the cliff area from upper left and to the right.

absolute dating are then fed across to comparative dating. Once certain fossils and their rocks are aged in this way, the dating can be used for similar specimens in other locations and for smaller timescales on a day-to-day basis.

Above: Trilobite fossils, such as this specimen found in Montana, USA, are useful for dating the Cambrian rocks prominent in some of the geology of this state.

Below: The limestone and shale cliffs at Gros Morne National Park, Newfoundland, Canada, define the boundary between the Cambrian and Ordovician Periods.

Palaeomagnetism

As some types of rocks formed, tiny iron-rich particles in their minerals were affected by the Earth's natural magnetic field. The field made the particles line up, like miniature compass needles. It is known that the planet's magnetic field has varied through time, both in strength and orientation, as the North and South Poles 'wandered' (and still do today). Sometimes the field even flipped or reversed as North became South and vice versa. All these changes are preserved in certain rocks, usually of volcanic origin. The sequences of changes are known, and fossils found in sedimentary rocks above or below the volcanic ones can be matched into the sequence. This gives another form of dating, known as palaeomagnetism.

Below: Iron ore displaying black areas of massive magnetite, and silvery quartz.

FOSSILS AND EVOLUTION

The general notion of evolution has been around for more than two thousand years. Fossils are one of the key areas of evidence supporting the theory of evolution, which is a cornerstone of the modern life sciences.

'The crust of the Earth with its imbedded remains must not be looked at as a well-filled museum, but as a poor collection made at hazard and at rare intervals.' Charles Darwin, Conclusion to *On The Origin of Species by Means of Natural Selection* (1859).

Aristotle (384–322 BC) of Ancient Greece vaguely mentioned what he called a hierarchy or ladder of life, with Man (humans) at the top. In these writings he perhaps foresaw some kind of evolutionary process. Many other natural philosophers mused on the idea of a time before humans, when different kinds of animals and plants lived. Some even suggested that kinds or species or living things were not fixed and unchanging – that is, they evolved. The notion gained ground in the early 1800s when experts such as Georges Cuvier began to accept that there had been previous extinctions. However at this time species were still

Above: German biologist Ernst Haeckel (1834–1919). Haeckel was greatly influenced by Darwin's work on evolution, although he remained suspicious about natural selection as a means of determining survival.

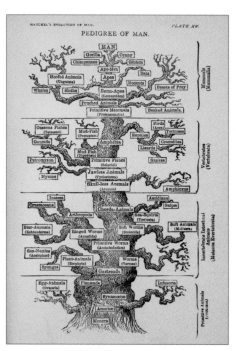

Above: An extract from Haeckel's work The Evolution of Man: a popular exposition of the principal points of human ontogeny and phylogeny, *published in 1879. Haeckel believed in a link between phylogeny – the concurrent changes demonstrated by a group of organisms – and biological development. However, his geneaological trees, such as the one shown above, often represented older ideas about the 'scale of being'. The above illustration shows the evolution of the human species, the 'pedigree of man', with the trunk representing a complete and linear line of progress from higher to lower forms.*

Below: Darwin's revolutionary theories about evolution were subject to both outrage and ridicule in certain quarters upon going into print. This cartoon shows a gorilla protesting of Darwin (shown right, holding his book On The Origin of Species*): "That man wants to claim my pedigree. He says he is one of my descendants." Henry Bergh, co-founder of the Society for the Prevention of Cruelty to Animals (shown middle), replies: "Now, Mr Darwin, how could you insult him so?"*

seen as never-changing between creation and extinction, according to teachings derived from the Bible.

The 'great book'

The idea of evolution smashed onto the scene in 1859 when English naturalist Charles Darwin published *On The Origin of Species by Means of Natural Selection*. Darwin argued that most living things produce too many offspring for all to survive the struggle for existence. Organisms struggle against the weather and physical conditions, against enemies and predators and similar problems, and against the limits of vital needs such as food, shelter or living space. The offspring which survive are those best suited or adapted to conditions of the time. This happens because not all offspring are identical. They naturally vary slightly. The variation usually

comes from genes, which are units of inheritance, like 'instructions' for how a living thing develops and functions. In sexual reproduction, genes from the parents are shuffled into different combinations for different offspring. Some of the offspring possess certain features or characters which other offspring lack.

Sexual reproduction and genetic variation provide the 'raw material' on which evolution acts. If a certain organism's features are an aid to survival, and are also inherited by its offspring, then the offspring are better adapted to the prevailing conditions. They have a better chance of survival. And so on, generation after generation.

Change with time

Darwin proposed that over very long time periods, as conditions and environments altered, certain kinds or species of living things gradually changed or evolved into different ones. Two chapters of *The Origin* dealt with fossils. Darwin realized that fossils represented excellent evidence for his ideas. They were remains of living things which had lost the struggle for survival. They died out as conditions changed, to be replaced by newer, better adapted forms. And this is a key point. Sooner or later, environmental conditions, such as the climate, begin to change. So living things are always playing 'catch-up' by evolving to fit the new conditions, even as that environment continues to alter.

Above: Scientists at Beijing University attempt to extract fragments of DNA from a large fossilized dinosaur egg.

Left: Organisms trapped in amber, like this spider (left), are helping palaeontologists in their endeavour to extend the DNA database from living to extinct organisms. The idea is that this will help them to clarify evolutionary relationships between genera and species.

A long long time

In his great book, Darwin was cautious about time spans. Many people of his period believed the literal truth of the Bible, which led to the calculation that Earth was created in the year 4004 BC. Darwin saw that the formation of fossils according to the theory of evolution would need much longer. He estimated Earth's age at up to 400 million years. He was also extremely aware of the chance-ridden nature of fossilization, and the random nature and huge gaps in the fossil record. So he warned that fossils were unlikely to show complete and gradual evolutionary sequences – there would be many gaps and jumps.

Below: Charles Darwin (1809–1882).

In the early 1970s, Stephen Jay Gould (1941–2002) and Niles Eldridge (1943–) proposed a modified version of Darwin's original idea. Based on the fossil record, they suggested that many organisms go through long periods of stability or stasis, when conditions remain relatively constant. Then there is a brief period of change, when new species rapidly appear, before stability again. This twist on Darwinism is known as punctuated equilibrium, or 'evolution by jerks', in comparison to the traditional 'evolution by creeps'.

Acceptance

Many ordinary people were outraged by Darwin's ideas, which seemed to fly in the face of religious ethic. But most scientists quickly saw how his proposals fitted with many strands of evidence. These included the similarities between various groups of living things, leading to how they are grouped or classified, and the evidence of changing fossils through time. Since Darwin's day many more strands of evidence have supported the idea of evolution. They include the basic nature of genes, and the structure of the chemical DNA that forms them, which is shared by nearly all living things. Some genes that control basic biochemical pathways, such as breaking apart energy-rich food substances to obtain energy for life processes, are found in identical form throughout vast numbers of hugely varied organisms. This is powerful evidence for the evolutionary process and the relatedness of living things.

CLASSIFICATION OF FOSSILS

For a long time, naming and classifying living things, and their fossils, was based on a system devised in the mid-18th century. However recent years have seen the rise of a newer system, which its supporters contend is based more on logic and less on judgement, known as cladistical analysis.

Most fossil-hunters name their finds according to a system devised in 1758 by Swedish-born plant biologist Carolus Linnaeus (Carl von Linné, 1707–1778). In his vast work *Systema Naturae* Linnaeus proposed that each kind or species of living thing should have two names. The first was its genus name – a genus being a group of similar or closely related species. The second name was unique to the species. From about 1780 the Linnaean system was gradually applied to fossils as well as living or extant species. So one of the genus names for certain kinds of shellfish called brachiopods (lampshells) which are common as fossils is *Lingula*. Individual species include *Lingula gredneri, L. anatina, L. cornea*, and dozens of others. Genus and species names are usually printed in *italics*, while names of other groups, like classes or orders, are not.

The origins of names
Usually the scientific names for living things and fossils are derived from Latin or another ancient language. They are international and recognized

Below: Carolus Linnaeus (1707–1778), from a portrait completed after the death of the 'Founder of Taxonomy'.

Above: For many years experts have debated: whether modern-day birds evolved from dinosaurs. In recent years the evidence has supported the answer 'Yes', and has also shown that feathers are not the unique possession of birds, as was once believed. Fossils of tyrannosaurs recently discovered in China show that these great predators had a partial covering of fine, downy feathers. A much smaller feathered dinosaur, Microraptor gui, is shown right.

by scientists all around the world, no matter what their own spoken or written languages. The meaning of a name may be based on a particular feature of the genus or species concerned, or perhaps where it is found, or who first discovered it.

Taxonomy
Linnaeus' binomial nomenclature (giving two names as a unique identification) has been extended and refined into a hierarchy of classification for all living things. The science of classifying organisms, living or extinct, is known as taxonomy, and its basic unit or 'building block' is the species. The species included in the same genus are selected by studying similarities and differences. The same is done with genera when they are grouped into a family, and so on, into larger groups. The biggest or topmost groups are kingdoms. Working from the top down:

• Kingdom
• Phylum (animals) / Division (plants)
• Class
• Order
• Family
• Genus
• Species

Levels of identification

The level of identification for a fossil, within the hierarchy of groups, varies hugely – according to practical considerations, amount of expertise, resources available, and scientific needs. Some amateur palaeontologists consider the label 'trilobite' is enough for a particular specimen. This is the everyday version of the scientific name for the class Trilobita. However other enthusiasts with more time and resources may wish to attempt a more accurate identification, perhaps even down to species level, such as:

Kingdom Animalia
Phylum Arthropoda
Class Trilobita
Order Phacopida
Family Calymenidae
Genus *Calymene*
Species *Calymene blumenbachii*

Below: The name of the trilobite Calymene blumenbachii *may be rather a mouthful, so in England it has the nickname of the 'Dudley bug' after the Midlands region where this fossil species is especially common.*

Traditional classification

Birds are a separate and higher rank (a Class) than dinosaurs (an Order).

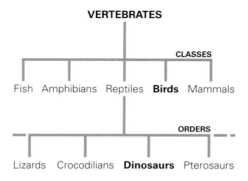

Above: Taking the classification of dinosaurs and birds as an example, we can see how the organization of animal groups differs radically in the traditional and cladistic methods. In the former, Birds are given the rank of class, equivalent to that of Reptiles. Dinosaurs are a subgroup of Reptiles, generally with the rank of order (Dinosauria). In cladistical analysis (shown right), Birds have a much lower rank than Dinosaurs, and are in fact part of the dinosaur group or clade.

Cladistics

From the 1960s, a different method of grouping living and extinct organisms has gradually been taking over from the traditional Linnaean version, especially among professional biologists, palaeontologists and life scientists. It is known as the cladistic method of phylogenetic systematics. It was devised by German biologist and expert on flies, Willi Hennig (1913–1976).

In the Linnaean system, the features or traits used to group organisms are often a matter of discussion or opinion. In cladistics, these features are specially identified as synapomorphies or 'unique derived characters'. Each unique derived character of feature arose only once. Descendants of the ancestor in which the character arose all share it. They, and only they, form a group known as a clade. This is an evolution-based group – all members of a clade are descended from the same common ancestor. As evolution continues, different derived characteristics evolve, so clades split

Left: Computers are massively powerful aids for comparing the features and relatedness of both living organisms and fossils, especially using the cladistic approach.

Cladistic view

Birds appear as a sub-group within the dinosaurs clade.

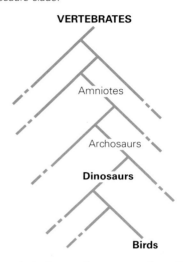

into subclades, and so on, and on. This creates the family tree type format shown above.

Cladograms

For example, assume that birds evolved from small, meat-eating dinosaurs. Then birds should be included within the dinosaur clade, as part of it. In the Linnaean system, birds are a separate and in fact larger group than dinosaurs. Birds are the class Aves, while dinosaurs are the order Dinosauria. Cladistics uses branching diagrams known as cladograms to show the evolutionary relationships between groups of organisms. The diagrams show branching points where new derived characteristics, and therefore new groupings, appear. This testable system is less prone to opinions and errors than the Linnaean version, and its administrative logic can be applied to other areas of life besides science. However for most practical and everyday purposes, the overall groupings of the Linnaean system are still in use.

Right: Limpets are included within the gastropod group, and given the genus name Patella, due to their similarity in shape to the human kneecap bone of this name.

FAMOUS FOSSILS

Fossils become famous for various reasons, such as scientific significance, scarcity or size. On the negative side, some specimens are more infamous or notorious, with links to tales of skulduggery, fossil-rustling and similar underhand tactics.

What makes a fossil famous? Usually, a mixture of reasons. The specimen might open up a whole new area of science, for example, by establishing a major and previously unsuspected group of extinct organisms. Its discovery could be a tale of romance and adventure, with fossil-hunters braving danger and taking risks to bring home their prize. The find might set a new record as the biggest, smallest or oldest of its kind. Or the fossil could turn up in a very unexpected place, chanced upon by a keen amateur who is suddenly catapulted into the media spotlight.

Conodonts

Tiny fossils commonly known as Conodonts or 'cone-teeth' resemble various tooth-like structures – long single fangs; many teeth in a line, like a crocodile's jaw; rows of spikes like teeth on a comb, either curved or straight; and other variations. Many are the size of sand grains and their wonderful shapes and arrangements can only be appreciated through a powerful hand lens or binocular microscope. These items are a common find in marine sediments worldwide during most of the Palaeozoic Era. They remained a mystery until the 1980s, when whole animals were

Below: The fossil Hallucigenia sparsa, *now held to have been a type of worm, found in The Burgess Shales, British Columbia.*

Above: Tooth-like conodont fossils from the Silurian Period, discovered in Russia. The real nature of these tiny yet intricate objects remained a mystery for centuries.

found which probably possessed them. A conodont creature resembled a long, slim fish or eel, roughly finger-sized or smaller, with two large eyes and blocks of muscles along the body. The conodont 'teeth' were arranged in the throat or neck region, but not in the jaws. Conodont creatures seem unrelated to any other groups of marine animals, living or extinct.

Hallucigenia

One of the best-known yet most puzzling creatures from the fossils in the 530 million-year-old Burgess Shales is *Hallucigenia*. It was described in 1977 as a surreal creature from a dreamworld – a long and vaguely worm-like body, blob-like head and narrow curved tail (or the reverse), seven pairs of stiff spines below for walking, and a row of about seven wavy tentacles above, each possibly tipped with a pincer-like 'mouth' for

feeding. However further finds shed more light on *Hallucigenia*. In 1991 a revised reconstruction showed the original version had been upside down. The twin rows of spines pointed upwards for protection. There were twin rows of tentacles too, not one. These pointed downwards and the 'mouths' were in fact feet used for walking. Hallucigenia may have been a very early type of onychophoran or velvet-worm, a group which includes *Peripatus* and still survives today, mainly in tropical rainforests.

Dimetrodon

Names are important for fossil-hunters. *Dimetrodon* was a three-metre-long predator from the Early Permian Period, some 280 million years ago. It had long fang-like teeth and a 'sail' of skin rising from its back, held up by long rods of bone. Its remains are plentiful in the fossil-rich 'Red Beds' of Texas, and have also been found in Oklahoma and in Europe. This powerful and impressive predator is often called a 'dinosaur'.

But it was not. It lived 50 million years before the first known dinosaurs. It belonged to a reptile group known as the pelycosaurs, which were the dominant large land animals of the time. The pelycosaurs were in turn part of the group known as synapsids or 'mammal-like reptiles'.

Mosasaurus

This fossil is mentioned several times in this book. It comprises parts of the skull, jaws and teeth of a large marine reptile. The remains were found in a chalk mine near Maastricht, Netherlands in 1770. In 1808 they were called *Mosasaurus* by Georges Cuvier, after the local region of the River Meuse. They led the renowned and influential Cuvier to a new proposal for the time, that many creatures had become extinct in previous catastrophes. Following many more similar finds, mosasaurs are now regarded as a group of large predatory sea reptiles from the Cretaceous Period. Some reached 15m/49ft in length. Their closest living relatives

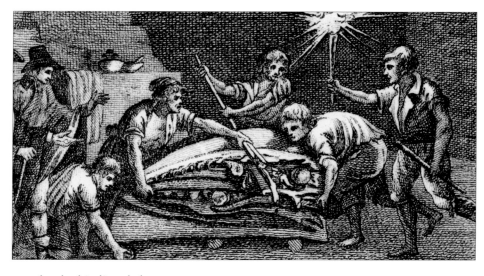

may be the big lizards known as monitors, such as the Nile monitor and Komodo dragon.

Forgeries

In 1912 remains of a human-like skull and ape-like jawbone were found at Piltdown, East Sussex, England. Experts hailed a marvellous new species of early human, *Eoanthropus dawsoni*. In 1953 careful scientific

Above: An engraving depicting the excavation of Mosasaurus *near Maastricht, published in a natural history study of the area in 1799.*

analysis revealed 'Piltdown Man' as a hoax. The 'fossils' were part of a amalgamation of a mediaeval human skull and an old orang-utan jawbone and chimpanzee tooth stained to match in colour. Piltdown still serves as a stark warning to over-zealous fossil sleuths everywhere.

Evidence of parental care

The parrot-beaked dinosaur *Psittacosaurus* from the Early Cretaceous Period is well known from many fossil finds in Asia. In 2004 a new discovery from Liaoning, China showed an adult *Psittacosaurus* surrounded by up to 34 part-grown youngsters. The amazing conclusion is that young from several parents formed a 'creche' that was looked after by one adult, perhaps while the others were feeding. These types of exciting discoveries allow us to reconstruct the behaviour of extinct animals with greater detail, showing that some dinosaurs were far from slow, stupid, simple beasts.

Below: Psittacosaurus had a hooked beak for snipping off vegetation and rows of crushing cheek teeth.

*Above and below: Two modern-day reptiles, the Nile monitor (*Varanus niloticus, *below left) and Komodo dragon (*Varanus komodoensis,

below right), may be closely related to prehistoric reptilian mosasaurs such as the species Platycarpus ictericus *(above).*

LIVING FOSSILS

Fossils cannot come to life, of course. But the close similarity of extant organisms to extinct ones has led to the concept of the 'living fossil'. This applies to plants and animals, but caution is needed when drawing conclusions from what may be misleading superficial comparisons.

The term 'living fossil' is something of a misnomer. Its usual implication is that exactly the same kind of plant or animal which was alive millions of years ago is still alive today. This is only partly true. Usually it is members of the same group which survive, such as a family or genus, rather than the actual species. However the survivors are largely unchanged from their cousins of millions of years ago.

Horsetails
The simple, flowerless plants called horsetails include the genus *Equisetum*, with about 20 species around the world. They are common 'weeds' of disturbed ground, each with a tall stem bearing whorls of

Left and below: Pictures from fossil horsetail specimens (left) display remarkable similarity with living species (below), even to the number of leaf-ribs in each whorl.

slim leaves like the ribs on an upside-down umbrella. Horsetails belong to the plant group called sphenopsids. They were far larger and more common in ancient times, with types such as *Equisetites*, *Asterophyllites* and *Calamites*. Their growths formed much of the vast Carboniferous forests and became preserved in coal.

Maidenhairs (ginkgos)
The maidenhair tree *Ginkgo biloba* is the only living species of a large group that flourished from the Early Permian through to the Tertiary Periods. Ginkgoes were especially common during the Jurassic, when giant dinosaurs walked among them and browsed their leaves. Today's maidenhair tree grows to 30m/130ft in height and has the characteristic fan-shaped leaves of its group. It was cultivated in the gardens of palaces and temples of Ancient China, its geographical home. In the early 18th century it was 'discovered' by European plant collectors and is now an ornamental park and street tree in many parts of the world.

Magnolias
The group known as angiosperms or flowering plants, which today includes familiar flowers, herbs, blossoms and broadleaved or deciduous trees, arose in the Cretaceous Period. Among the early types were magnolias, dating back more than 110 million years. Today's main ornamental types, with their large white and perhaps pink-tinged early blooms, are derived from Ancient Chinese species. Other flowers and trees which have changed little since Cretaceous times include waterlilies, planes and laurels.

Above: A reconstruction of a prehistoric brachiopod (of the Terebratula *genus). Modern day relatives of these mollusc-like creatures look very similar to fossils (see opposite).*

Lampshells (brachiopods)
From the outside, a lampshell or brachiopod ('arm-foot') looks similar to a bivalve mollusc such as a mussel, clam or oyster. However the two are very different. Lampshells have been

Above and below: Reconstructions of Cretaceous magnolias (below) show the same flower arrangement as the modern day Magnolia *species, such as this* Magnolia reliata *(above).*

*Above: This Jurassic brachiopod fossil (*Lingula beani*) exhibits a shiny lustre created by its mineral content (calcium phosphate). It has a characteristic lampshell shape.*

around since the Cambrian Period, more than 500 million years ago. Their two shells are usually very similar but one is larger than the other, and each shell is symmetrical from side to side (unlike most bivalves). More than 30,000 kinds of fossil lampshells are known. There are only 350 living species and most, such as *Lingula*, are filter-feeders in the deep sea.

Nautiluses

The few living species of pearly nautilus (including *Nautilus pompilius*) are the only remnants of a vast group of molluscs that were very common predators in Palaeozoic seas. Today's living nautiluses are large-eyed, curly-shelled, many-tentacled hunters of fish and other prey. They dwell in the deep sea. But there were more than 2,500 prehistoric types including straight-shelled nautiluses more than five metres long. Nautiloids are sometimes confused with ammonoids and belemnoids, which were also cephalopod molluscs and also extinct. Their living cousins are octopuses, squid and cuttlefish.

Tuataras

The tuatara resembles an iguana lizard. But it belongs to a very different group of reptiles called rhynchocephalians, which thrived at the time of the early dinosaurs, some 250–200 million years ago in the Triassic Period. Rhynchocephalians like *Scaphonyx* of the Middle Triassic were bulky plant-eaters almost two metres long, weighing nearly 100kg/220lb. Only two tuatara species now survive, on rocky islands off the coast of New Zealand.

They grow to about 60cm/24in long and come out of their burrows at night to feed on worms, insects and spiders.

*Above and below: The 'relict reptile', the tuatara (*Sphenodon, *above), gives a rare and valuable insight into the evolution of its group, the rhynchocephalians (below) that were common during the Triassic Period.*

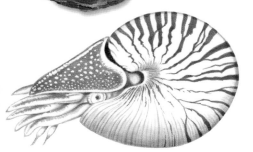

Left: Millions of fossil nautiloid specimens (like the example left) confirm the close relationship with the living representatives of the deep sea, such as Nautilus pompilius *(below).*

An extinct species returns to life

The coelacanths are bony fish which have 'lobe-fins' (Osteichthyes) – a fleshy muscular base or stalk to each fin. They belong to the group Sarcopterygii, in contrast to the Actinopterygii or 'ray fins', the group that contains the vast majority of bony fish. Coelacanths first appeared way back in the Devonian Period. They reached 3m/10.5ft in length during the Early Cretaceous Period but faded away. Thought to be extinct from about 70 million years ago, a living coelacanth was caught off the coast of East Africa in 1938. Several specimens have been obtained since, and a second species, the Indonesian coelacanth, was discovered in the late 1990s. These fish grow to about 1.8m/6.5ft long, live in deep water, eat crabs and similar prey, and have a curious three-lobed tail.

Below: A reconstruction of an ancient (left) and modern day (right) coelacanth. These fish have many intriguing features, including a small tassel-like addition to the two main lobes of the caudal (tail) fin.

FOSSILS AND US

Since ancient times, people have speculated that we, as humans, evolved from some type of ape-like ancestors. The search for fossils of our ancestors and extinct cousins is one of the most exciting and controversial areas of palaeontology.

More than 2,000 years ago Aristotle of Ancient Greece wrote that 'some animals share the properties of Man and the quadrupeds, as the ape, the monkey and the baboon'. When Charles Darwin proposed the theory of evolution by natural selection in 1859, he was vilified for daring to suggest that our ancestors were some kinds of monkeys or apes. In fact, in *On The Origin of Species*, his only comment about human evolution was that 'Much light will be thrown on the origin of man and his history'.

The quest for 'missing links'

In 1856 some human-like bones were discovered by workmen mining limestone in a cave in the Neander Valley near Dusseldorf, Germany. The skull has a low brow, very thick bones and heavy jaw. Some experts dismissed it as 'an individual affected with idiocy and rickets'. But others began to think seriously that remains of ancient humans, including our ancestors, were preserved in rocks. The search for 'missing link' fossils had begun.

Below: Donald Johanson, discoverer of 'Lucy', with a plaster cast of her skull.

Above: Cast of an original skull of the 'Taung child', Australopithecus africanus, *discovered by Raymond Dart in Taung, Cape Province, South Africa.*

Gathering evidence

One of the first major discoveries was made by Dutch scientist Eugene Dubois near Trinil, Java in 1890–92. It consisted of part of an upper skull, a piece of jawbone with tooth, and a thigh bone (femur), and soon became known as 'Java Man'. Dubois named it *Pithecanthropus erectus*, and stated: 'I consider it a link connecting apes and men.' In 1927 a team led by Canadian anatomist Davidson Black excavated 'Dragon Bone Hill' at Zhoukoudian (Chou'kou'tien) near Beijing, China. They found many bones of another missing link which they named *Sinanthropus pekinensis*, 'Peking Man'. With continual revision of fossils and their names, both of these discoveries are now included within the species *Homo erectus*. Meanwhile in 1925 Australian anatomist Raymond Dart named a much more ape-like skull from Southern Africa, informally known as the 'Taung child', as *Australopithecus africanus*.

No longer missing

Gradually more fossils came to light of prehistoric humans. One of the most celebrated finds was 'Lucy' – the two-fifths complete skeleton of a species known as *Australopithecus afarensis*, found in Hadar, Ethiopia. It was

discovered in 1974 by Donald Johanson and represented a small 1m/3.5ft-tall ape-like creature from more than three million years ago, which could walk upright almost like us. Many experts now believe that 'Lucy' was in fact a male and have renamed him 'Lucifer'. Further finds in the 1990s and 2000s include even more ape-like creatures from even longer ago. They include *Ardipthecus ramidus* from Aramis, Ethiopia, whose fossils are almost four and a half million years old, and *Orrorin tugenensis*, a more controversial discovery from Kenya, which is some six million years old. Ethiopia was again the site of a remarkable discovery in September 2006: the skeleton of a 3 year-old child, more or less complete, was uncovered by scientists based at the Max Planck Institute for Evolutionary Anthropology, Leipzig, Germany. Although older than Lucy, the child was also a member of *A. afarensis*, and her lower limbs again suggested a

Below: Dr G.H.R. von Koenigswald examining the upper jaw of Pithecanthropus robustus, *once known as Java Man. This species was later assigned to the genus* Homo *as an example of* Homo erectus.

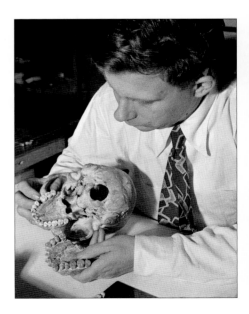

The 'hobbit humans'

In 2004 an astonishing find on the island of Flores, Indonesia, overturned many ideas about recent human evolution. It was believed that since the extinction of the last Neanderthal and *Homo erectus* people by 25,000 years ago, our own species *Homo sapiens* was the only hominid on the planet. However it seems that as recently as 13,000 years ago, diminutive humans lived on Flores. Only one metre tall, they are known as *Homo floresiensis*. The skulls of these mini-people are hardly the size of grapefruits.

Yet relatively sophisticated stone tools and the remains of charred animal bones have also been found at the site. This raises huge questions about brain size related to the intelligence needed for making tools and using fire. The size reduction of species when confined to an island habitat – a phenomenon known as 'island dwarfism' – appears many times in the fossil record, and can be seen in mammoths and elephants. However the conclusion that the Flores remains represent an entirely separate species of human is disputed until, as palaeontologists tend to say in furtherance of their profession, 'further evidence is forthcoming'.

Below: Debate surrounds the Flores hominids. Was the main species, reconstructed below, small but otherwise normal, or suffering from some kind of growth malformation?

capacity to walk upright. Her ape-like arms and shoulders, however, indicated that she may also have spent much of her life sheltering in trees.

'Found links'

Apart from fossils, the evidence of genes, DNA and other molecules within the bodies of ourselves and chimpanzees show that they are our closest living relatives. It is estimated that humans and chimps split from a common ancestor some seven or eight million years ago. Our 'branch' of the evolutionary tree makes up the family Hominidae. Some palaeontologists contend that it includes 20 or more species, many overlapping in time and place, especially in Africa. Others propose as few as eight species. It seems that the 'cradle of human evolution' was indeed Africa, that upright walking began several million years ago, that tool use dates back more than two million years ago, and that brain size has tended to increase through all this time.

DIRECTORY OF FOSSILS

No single bookbound collection of fossil images could ever incorporate every group and individual kind of organism that has left its record in the rocks. However, one can strive to create a soundly representative compilation of the common and recognizable forms – importantly, from different times and places around the world – plus a few glimpses of the most rare and precious of all fossils.

The following pages include many groups of organisms which are familiar to hordes of amateur fossil enthusiasts, such as ferns, sponges, marine molluscs and trilobites, but which, nevertheless, retain their own beauty, fascination, and importance, especially in the context of a local collection. There are no apologies for including a few tantalizing examples of momentous finds that would make any palaeontologist gasp with awe and glow with a sense of achievement.

The directory is organized into three major traditional groupings: plants, invertebrate (mostly non-chordate) animals, and vertebrate (mostly chordate) animals. Each grouping is generally subdivided into the conventional taxonomic assemblages, such as, taking members of the phylum Mollusca as an example, the bivalves and ammonites. However, as noted earlier in this book, there are disagreements among experts about the extent or separation of certain groups. And the ways in which these groups are ranked are being continually altered and refined with the aid of scientific scrutiny and the logical framework provided by the system of cladistical taxonomy (see Classification of Fossils in the previous chapter).

Left: The Dinosaur Provincial Park in Alberta, Canada, a designated World Heritage Site, demonstrates the 'pulling power' of important fossils.

EARLY PLANTS

The very first life on Earth was mainly microscopic. The first multicelled plants appeared in the sea, perhaps around one billion years ago. They are usually known as algae – the simplest category of plants, lacking true roots and leaves and reproducing by simple spores instead of flowers and seed-containing fruits. Well-known algae today include sea-lettuces, wracks, kelps, oarweeds and dulses.

Mixed algal–Chaetetes deposit

Below: This specimen, which incorporates algae and Chaetetes depressus, is from varied Late Carboniferous limestones that were found on inland cliff deposits exposed at the River Avon Gorge in Clifton, Bristol, south-west England.

Chaetetes has long been something of a mystery. It has been interpreted as a coral of the tabulate (flat-topped or table-like) group, or an encrusting sponge (poriferan) of the coralline demosponge type. Specimens are often combined with encrusting algae rich in the mineral calcium carbonate, making varied forms of limestone. Similar fossil structures have been called stromatoporoids, or 'layered pores', and these, in turn, show similarities to a relatively newly identified group of living sponges – the encrusting sclerosponges. So *Chaetetes* may well have been a sponge rather than a coral. However, in fossils it is often difficult to differentiate between the algal, poriferan and coral elements. Similar algal–*Chaetetes* carbonate accumulations from the Ely Basin, dating to the Mid to Late Carboniferous, are found along the western edge of North America. 'Chaetetes Bands' are also common in northern England and several European regions, including Germany and Poland.

Name: Algal–Chaetetes limestone
Meaning: ––
Grouping: Encrusting alga (plants) and *Chaetetes* (probably poriferan or sponge)
Informal ID: Algal-sponge-coral accumulation, 'sea floor stone'
Fossil size: Specimen 6cm/2⅜in across
Reconstructed size: Some formations cover many square kilometres
Habitat: Warm, shallow seas
Time span: Mainly Mesozoic, 250–65 million years ago
Main fossil sites: Europe, North America
Occurrence: ◆ ◆

Carboniferous algal deposit

Below: This Carboniferous structure may be a cyst – a tough-walled container enclosing the thallus, or main body, of the alga, possibly a frond. What looks like the 'leaf' of a seaweed-type alga is known as the frond, the 'stem' is termed the stipe, and some types have 'root'-like structures, known as holdfasts, to anchor them to rocks.

Like many simple plants, some types of algae do not contain hard materials, such as lignin (as in wood), nor do they produce tough, resistant structures, such as nuts or pollen grains. Usually they are preserved in detail only if they incorporate some type of resistant mineral, such as silica or chalk/limestone (calcium carbonate or calcareous minerals, see opposite) into their bodies, or thalli. In some examples, the encysted form shows a tough wall developed to resist drying or similar adverse conditions (see left). However, algal fossils have an immense time span extending back to the Precambrian Period, more than 540 million years ago, and have been used as index or indicator fossils to date marine deposits, especially in the search for petroleum oil.

Name: Carboniferous algal deposit
Meaning: ––
Grouping: Alga, Cyanophyte
Informal ID: Seaweed
Fossil size: 5cm/2in across
Reconstructed size: Whole plant up to 1m/3¼ft
Habitat: Warm seashores and shallow seas
Time span: Precambrian, before 540 million years ago, to today
Main fossil sites: Worldwide
Occurrence: ◆ ◆

Coelosphaeridium

Name: *Coelosphaeridium*
Meaning: Little hollow spheres
Grouping: Alga, green alga
Informal ID: Ball-shaped stony seaweed
Fossil size: Individual specimen 7cm/2¾in across
Reconstructed size: As above, forming large beds of many square metres
Habitat: Warm seashores and shallow seas
Time period: Mainly Palaeozoic, 540–250 million years ago
Main fossil sites: Northern Europe
Occurrence: ◆ ◆

Calcareous alga such as *Coelosphaeridium* lay down deposits of chalky or limestone minerals (calcium carbonate) and jelly-like substances within and sometimes around their tissues. This gives the plant a stiff, stony feel and aids preservation. *Coelosphaeridium* is common in certain parts of northern Europe, especially Scandinavia. It forms mixed beds along with other algae, such as *Mastopora* and *Cyclocrinus* (named from its original identification as a sea-lily or crinoid, a member of the echinoderm group, but now regarded by some authorities as a siphonean alga), and with various encrusting animal invertebrates, such as sponges and corals.

Below: These fossilized remains of the algal 'cells' of Coelosphaeridium *are from Ringsaker, Norway, where they occur in large accumulations. They date back to the Ordovician Period, about 450 million years ago. The outer wall resembles bark with a pattern of radiating spoke-like elements enclosing a central chamber, where the radial structure is less defined.*

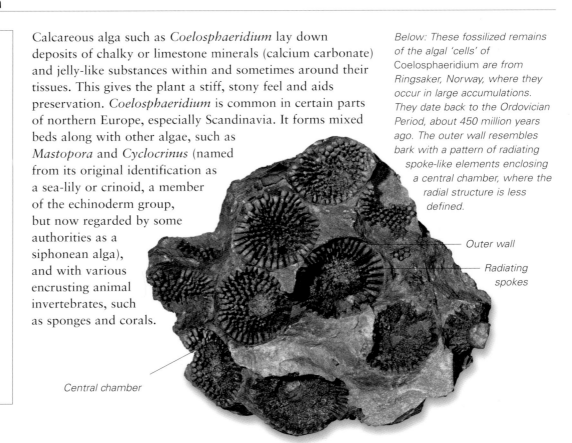

Outer wall

Radiating spokes

Central chamber

Algal stromatolitic limestone (mixed composition)

Name: Algal stromatolitic limestone
Meaning: Stromatolite = 'layer stone'
Grouping: Algae
Informal ID: As above, 'seaweed rock'
Fossil size: Specimen 19cm/7½in across
Reconstructed size: Large deposits can extend for kilometres
Habitat: Warm seashores and shallow seas
Time period: Precambrian, before 540 million years ago, to today
Main fossil sites: Worldwide
Occurrence: ◆ ◆

Fossilized stromatolites, or 'layered stones', were once thought to be produced by tiny animals known as protozoans, or by inorganic (non-living) processes of mineral deposition. However, comparison with rocky deposits found along many warm seashores today, famously Shark Bay in Western Australia, reveal that these humped or mound-like structures, generally varying in size from that of a tennis ball up to that of a family car, usually have an organic origin. Tiny threads of green algae and blue-green 'algae' (see Cyanobacteria, discussed earlier) thrive in tangled, low mats, covering themselves with slime and jelly for protection. These growths trap sand, silt and other sediments, as well as fragments of shell and other organic matter. New algal mats grow on top as the ones below harden, and slowly the mound builds up as a multi-layered stromatolite. In calm waters, the stromatolite shape is often rounded, resembling a burger bun, while strong currents cause them to elongate, like French baguettes (sticks), lying parallel to the current's direction.

Below: This specimen dates from the Late Carboniferous Period and is from Blaenavon, in Monmouth, Wales. The laminated, or layered, structure is typical of stromatolitic formations.

Laminated structure

Limestone

EARLY LAND PLANTS

Before the evolution of primitive land plants, some 440 million years ago, the land was rocky and barren except for mats of algae and mosses along the edge of the water. By about 400 million years ago vascular plants, such as the Rhyniales and Zosterophyllales, began to spread. These early plants reproduced by unleashing clouds of spores, in the manner of simpler plants, such as mosses and ferns, today.

Cooksonia

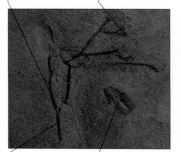

Y-shaped branching point | Terminal spore capsule

Stem | Eurypterid

Above: The presence of a eurypterid (sea-scorpion) in this sample, from the Upper Olney Limestone of Onondaga County, New York, USA, suggests that the rock was formed on the sea bed. So the plant had been transported and washed out to sea, perhaps by heavy rains.

One of the earliest and best-known vascular land plants appeared late in the Silurian Period. *Cooksonia* was a small and simple plant, yet it achieved worldwide distribution – although it is dominantly known from Eurasia and, especially, Great Britain. Its success may be largely due to its vascular system (see *Rhynia*, overleaf), which allowed water, minerals and sugars to be distributed throughout its entire body. *Cooksonia* had no leaves like modern plants, but it was probably green and photosynthesized (captured the sun's light energy) over its whole stem surface. It is recognizable by its characteristic smooth, Y-branching stems that end in spore capsules shaped like kidney beans.

Right: Features of Cooksonia *include the Y-shaped branching stem and the spore capsules (sporangia) borne singly at the end of each stem. Some specimens have just one branch forming a Y; others have five or more levels. The stems are smooth, rarely carrying surface features.*

Name: *Cooksonia*
Meaning: Named for Australian palaeobotanist Isabel Cookson
Grouping: Rhyniale, Rhyniacean
Informal ID: Simple vascular plant, early land plant
Fossil size: Smaller slab 4cm/1½in across
Reconstructed size: Entire height usually less than 10cm/4in
Habitat: Shores near rivers, lakes
Time period: Late Silurian to Devonian, 410–380 million years ago
Main fossil sites: Worldwide, especially Eurasia and Britain
Occurrence: ◆ ◆

Zosterophyllum

Branching point | Laterally clustered sporangia

A late Silurian vascular plant, like *Cooksonia* (above), *Zosterophyllum* is distinguished by having Y-like and also H-shaped branches, where each branch is divided into two equal stems. Each stem was smooth, and the spore capsules were clustered in the manner of a 'flower spike' towards the end of the stem but on the sides, rarely the tip. The capsules split along the sides, unfurling like a fern to release their spores. Nutrients were shared between stems by a network of underground root-like rhizomes. Plants such as *Zosterophyllum* were probably ancestral to the giant lycopods, or clubmosses, that dominated the coal swamps of the Carboniferous Period.

Left: Zosterophyllum *had its oval- or kidney-shaped sporangia (spore capsules) on short stalks, clustered in long arrays along the sides of the terminal stem, rather than at its end (as in* Cooksonia*).*

Name: *Zosterophyllum*
Meaning: Girded leaf
Grouping: Zosterophyllale, Zosterophyllacean
Informal ID: Simple vascular plant, early land plant
Fossil size: Specimen length (height) 4.5cm/1¾in
Reconstructed size: Entire height 25–30cm/10–12in
Habitat: Edges of lakes, slow rivers
Time period: Late Silurian to Middle Devonian, 410–370 million years ago
Main fossil sites: Worldwide
Occurrence: ◆ ◆

Gosslingia

Name: *Gosslingia*
Meaning: For Gosling
Grouping: Zosterophyllale, Gosslingian
Informal ID: Simple vascular plant, early land plant
Fossil size: Slab 4cm/ 1½in across
Reconstructed size: Height up to 50cm/20in
Habitat: Edges of lakes
Time period: Early Devonian, 400 million years ago
Main fossil sites: Throughout Europe
Occurrence: ◆ ◆

This fossilized remains of this early land plant show it to be smooth-stemmed with a distinguishing Y-shaped branching pattern. The sporangia (spore capsules) are scattered along the length of the stem on small side branches, rather than clustered at or near the end. In addition, some stem tips are coiled, much like those of a modern fern, in a form known as circinate. Many of these plants were washed downstream by floods and deposited in oxygen-deficient mud. These anaerobic conditions prevented decay and allowed the plants to fossilize as pyrite, or 'fool's gold' (known as pyritization), preserving in microscopic detail the cellular structure of the original plant as it was in life.

Below: Gosslingia *shows the typical Y-shaped branching pattern of many early plants. However, in this specimen, small lateral or side branches are also evident, some bearing sporangia.*

Sporangia (spore capsules)

Lateral branch

Main stem

Compsocradus

This genus of plant forms part of a group known as the iridopteridaleans, from the Mid to Late Devonian Period in Venezuela and the Carboniferous of China. The branches are whorled (grouped like the ribs of an umbrella) and vascularized for photosynthesis. Some of the uppermost branches divide up to six times before ending in curled tips, while others have paired spore capsules at their tips.

Right: Laterally compressed (squashed flat from side to side), this fossilized specimen of Sawdonia *shows its spiny nature. In life, the stems may have bunched together, possibly to form a prickly thicket that gave mutual support and protection and allowed the plants to reach greater heights.*

Sawdonia

Name: *Sawdonia*
Meaning: Saw-tooth
Grouping: Zosterophyllale, Sawdonian
Informal ID: Simple vascular plant, early land plant
Fossil size: 23cm/9in
Reconstructed size: Height up to 30cm/12in
Habitat: Shores
Time period: Early Devonian, 400 million years ago
Main fossil sites: Worldwide
Occurrence: ◆ ◆

Sawdonia is distinctly different from other early land plants in being covered with saw-toothed, spiny or scale-like flaps of tissue along its stems. However, these flaps of tissue were not vascularized – in other words, did not have fluid-transporting pipe-like vessels – and therefore cannot be considered as true leaves. Their function is not clear. They may have been spiky defences against early insect-like land animals. The presence on the flaps of stomata – tiny holes allowing the exchange of gases and water vapour between the inside of the plant and the surrounding air – suggests that they increased the photosynthetic surface area of the plant for greater capture of light energy. The sporangia of *Sawdonia* are found laterally (along the sides) and the branch tips are circinate, uncoiling like the head of a fern.

Stem branching

Saw-toothed tissue

FERNS, SEED FERNS

There are more than 11,000 species of fern today, making them the largest main group of plants after the flowering plants, or angiosperms. Like many other types of simpler plants, they reproduce by spores. Ferns first appeared in the Devonian, thrived through the Carboniferous, became less common during the Late Permian and the Middle Cretaceous, but underwent a resurgence during the Tertiary.

Psaronius, Pecopteris

Fern sporangia

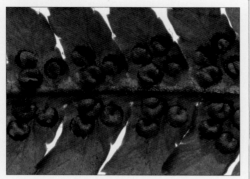

A fern's spore containers, or capsules, known as sporangia, sometimes look like rows of 'buttons' or 'kidneys' along the underside of the fern frond. These are the sporangia of the extant male fern *Dryopteris filix-mas*, a common woodland species. The protective scale which forms the outside of each sporangium is known as the indusium. This becomes grey as the spores ripen ready for release into the wind.

The identification and grouping of fern fossils is a very tricky subject, as exemplified by the preserved remains of fronds called *Pecopteris*. It was eventually discovered that these grew on tree ferns that had already received their own names, such as *Psaronius*, from the fossils of their strong, thick trunks. In addition, other parts of these plants, such as the rhizomes ('roots'), have also received yet more names. (The same problems have also arisen with seed ferns, see overleaf.) *Psaronius* was one of the most common tree ferns of Late Carboniferous and Early Permian times. It would have superficially resembled a modern palm tree, growing with a tall, straight, unbranched trunk and an umbrella-like crown of fronds. Small roots branching from the lower main stem, called adventitious roots, caused thickening of the lower trunk, which was known as the root mantle. This arrangement helped to stabilize the whole tree fern. *Psaronius* is thought to have grown on elevated and drier areas around the swamplands. Its dominance towards the end of the Carboniferous Period is associated with climate warming and the disappearance of flooded wetlands. It faded later in the Permian, when the climate became drier and hotter. To add to the confusion, some specimens of *Pecopteris* have been reassigned to the genus *Lobatopteris*, which is not a true fern but a member of a different plant group – the seed ferns (see opposite and overleaf).

Left: The genus Pecopteris *is plentiful and widespread in the fossil record. Some specimens are in excellent condition, but others are only fragments, making identification difficult. This has caused considerable confusion with several hundred species assigned to the genus in some listings. In most specimens, the leaflets had two or three subdivisions (see opposite) and were shaped like rectangles with rounded ends. The central vein, or midrib, gave off smaller side veins at right angles.*

Main leaflet (pinna) composed of paired subleaflets (pinnules)

Fragmented leaflets

Central stem or rachis

Name: *Psaronius*
Meaning: Of grey, in grey
Grouping: Monilophyte, Marattiale
Informal ID: Tree fern
Fossil size: —
Reconstructed size: Height up to 10m/33ft
Habitat: Elevated, drier areas of swampland
Time span: Late Carboniferous to Mid Permian, 310–270 million years ago
Main fossil sites: Worldwide
Occurrence: ◆ ◆ ◆

Name: *Pecopteris*
Meaning: Comb wing
Grouping: Monilophyte, Marattiale
Informal ID: Frond of tree fern such as *Psaronius*
Fossil size: Slab 10cm/ 4in long
Reconstructed size: Frond length to 1.5m/5ft
Habitat: See *Psaronius*
Time span: See *Psaronius*
Main fossil sites: Worldwide
Occurrence: ◆ ◆ ◆

Lobatopteris

Name: *Lobatopteris*
Meaning: Lobed wing
Grouping: Pteridosperm
Informal ID: Tree-like
seed fern
Fossil size: Slab 10cm/
4in long
Reconstructed size: Height
5m/16½ft
Habitat: Drier parts of
swampland
Time span: Carboniferous to
Permian, 320–270 million
years ago
Main fossil sites:
Northern Hemisphere
Occurrence: ◆ ◆

Part of the famous Mazon Creek fossils of central North America, *Lobatopteris* is an example of a common problem that occurs in palaeontology. Often, a genus name has to be changed at some later date, because new discoveries about its true nature and classification come to light as further finds are made. As a result, some species of *Pecopteris*, from the true ferns (see opposite), have now been renamed in the genus *Lobatopteris*, and reclassified as seed ferns, or pteridosperms (see overleaf). The whole plant would have resembled a sizable tree, growing several metres in height, and living in the drier, probably more elevated areas around the swamplands. Pteridosperms mostly had fern-like foliage, but they produce real seeds, as opposed to spores as in true ferns.

Right: This fossilized imprint shows a typical fern-like leaf, or frond, preserving the individual leaflets in detail. The central stem, or rachis, while not visible, is represented by a depression running along the middle.

Subleaflets

Leaflet

Central stem
depression

Ferns, fronds, leaves and leaflets

The parts of a typical fern commonly called leaves are also known as fronds. These may be smooth-edged and undivided, as in today's hart's-tongue fern. Alternatively, they may be deeply divided, or 'dissected', into many smaller sections, which are themselves subdivided, and so on, with a repeating pattern. The terminology associated with all these parts is complex, but in general:
• The frond is comparable to the whole leaf with its stalk, which grows up from the root area.
• The stalk of the frond is called the stipe.
• The rachis is the main stalk, or stem, that runs along the middle of the frond, from which the other parts branch to each side, often in simultaneous pairs or alternately.

Below: The unfurling frond or 'fiddlehead' of a male fern.

• The pinna, or leaflet, is one of these branches from the main stalk, or rachis, of the frond.
• Pinnules, or subleaflets, may branch from the stalk of the pinna. This is called a twice-divided, or twice-cut, frond.
• A pinnule may, in turn, have a lobed structure, giving a thrice-divided, or thrice-cut, frond.
• When the fronds are young, they are curled up in a spiral form and as they unfurl they are known as the fiddle-head.

With their changing shapes and detailed structures, ferns are often important as index, or marker fossils, helping to date the rock layers in which they are found.

Below: Oak ferns jostle for space with a familiar angiosperm, the violet (the genus Viola*).*

CLUBMOSSES (LYCOPODS)

The swamps of the Carboniferous represented perhaps the greatest accumulation of biomass (living matter) ever. We exploit these fossilized remains when burning coal and natural gas. Much of this wetland vegetation consisted of plants called lycopods (lycopsids), or clubmosses – some as tall as 50m/165ft. Clubmosses were not closely related to true mosses (Bryophytes, Musci) or to early ferns and seed ferns.

Baragwanathia

Name: *Baragwanathia*
Meaning: After Australian geologist William Baragwanath
Grouping: Lycopod, Baragwanathiale
Informal ID: Clubmoss
Fossil size: Slab height 10cm/4in
Reconstructed size: Plant height up to 25cm/10in
Habitat: Damp lowland areas, floodplains
Time span: Late Silurian to Early Devonian, 420–400 million years ago
Main fossil sites: Australia
Occurrence: ◆

This curious and controversial plant is named in honour of William Baragwanath, who was the Director of the Geological Survey in the southern state of Victoria, Australia, from 1922 to 1943. William Baragwanath was born in the gold-mining town of Ballarat in 1878, the son of Cornish immigrants from the west of Britain lured to Australia in the hope of striking it rich in the booming gold fields of the time. The plant that bears his name is regarded by many experts as being a clubmoss, but from a very early time, more than 400 million years ago. This was when very few other land plants are known, and those that were present – such as *Cooksonia* (detailed earlier) – were much more primitive. In this context, 'primitive' means that it had fewer specialized features. *Baragwanathia* was first identified as imprints in rocks from the well-known Yea site in Victoria, Australia, and has since been discovered in other Australian localities. Dating methods put the remains at the Ludlovian Age of the Late Silurian Period, some 420 million years ago. The dating uses the fossils of graptolites, which are commonly found in sediments deposited in deep-water settings, and has been challenged by some authorities. However, it is possible that those plants of the great southern supercontinent of Gondwana were more advanced than their northern contemporaries.

Central stem

Clothing strip-like leaves give 'brush' effect

Leaves were borne at upright angle

Left: The stems of Baragwanathia were clothed in what are regarded as true leaves – which resembled small strips, narrow ribbons or spines – each up to 1cm/⅜in in length. The growth habit included branching horizontal stems, which also branched to give upright stems, growing to 10–25cm/4–10in in height. There were spore capsules in the axils – where the leaves joined the stem.

Living clubmosses

There are more than 1,000 species of extant (still living) clubmosses on the planet today. However, these are mostly smallish, low-growing, creeping plants, generally simple in form, and are most often to be found growing in the undergrowth, and they are merely a shadowy relict of their former glory in the Carboniferous Period when they could attain heights of up to 50m/165ft. Today's clubmosses resemble tough, tall mosses, but they possess the distinguishing feature of having a simple yet definite vascular system of vessels (tubes) to distribute water and nutrients around the plant. The spores are shed from spore-bearing leaves known as sporophylls. The species shown below is *Lycopodium annotinum*, commonly known as the 'stiff clubmoss'. It has narrow shoots comprised of tightly overlapping pointed leaves. When mature, it may grow to 30cm/1ft in height. Its favoured habitat is moist forest and thickets, and this species is particularly common in the foothills of Alberta, Canada.

Drepanophycus

Name: *Drepanophycus*
Meaning: Sickle plant
Grouping: Lycopod, Baragwanathiale
Informal ID: Clubmoss
Fossil size: Fossil slab 14cm/5½in long
Reconstructed size: Height 50cm/20in, rarely 1–2m/3¼–6½ft
Habitat: Moist settings, river and lake banks
Time span: Early Devonian to Carboniferous, 390–300 million years ago
Main fossil sites: Eurasia
Occurrence: ◆ ◆

The clubmoss *Drepanophycus* had a lowish 'creeping' form, evolved sometime in the Early Devonian Period and persisted through most of the Carboniferous, although as a genus it appears to have been restricted to the Northern Hemisphere. Some of these plants could attain several metres in height, although 50cm/20in was more usual. Each upright stem forked into two at an acute angle, perhaps more than once. The stem was covered with spiny, thorny or scale-like leaves, probably as a means of defence against insect predation. The leaves arose from the stem in a spiral pattern, although this was variable and at times they could appear whorled (emerging like the spokes of a wheel).

Right: The fossil shows the impression of Drepanophycus along with its spiny leaves. A characteristic feature of the genus is its thickened stem, which can reach several centimetres in diameter. This specimen is from the Devonian Old Red Sandstone of Rhineland, Germany.

Spiny leaves

Side fork

Thickened stem

Sigillaria

Name: *Sigillaria*
Meaning: Seal-like
Grouping: Lycopod, Lepidodendrale
Informal ID: Tree-like clubmoss
Fossil size: Slab size could not be confirmed
Reconstructed size: Height 20m/66ft, rarely 30m/ 100ft plus
Habitat: Moist settings, marshy forests
Time span: Early Carboniferous to Permian, 340–260 million years ago
Main fossil sites: North America, Europe
Occurrence: ◆ ◆

Sigillaria is a large, well-known clubmoss, known mainly from the Late Carboniferous Period. The genus varies in form, but most types were fairly tall, standing around 20m/66ft in height, yet also very sturdy – as much as 2m/6½ft across at the base. The main trunk tapered slowly with height and did not divide profusely, with many specimens sending out only a few arm-like side branches. The upper regions of the plant were covered with long, slim leaves, resembling blades of freshly growing grass, that grew directly from the main stem and fell away to leave behind characteristic leaf scars between the strengthening vertical ribs. The leaves were long and narrow – up to 1m/3¼ft long and only about 1cm/⅓in across. Some of the fossils known as *Stigmaria* may be preserved roots of *Sigillaria*.

Right: This section of Sigillaria trunk bears the distinctive 'seal'- or 'crab'-like leaf scars, from where the leaves grew straight out. Older leaves fell from the main trunk as the plant gained height, so most foliage was found in the upper region. Some types of Sigillaria are thought to have reached heights of 35m/115ft. This specimen comes from Carboniferous rocks near Barnsley, England.

Strengthening vertical ribs

Leaf scars

EARLY TREES – CYCADS

Plants can be divided into two groups. Sporophytes reproduce by spores (simple cells with no food store or protective coat). In spermatophytes, male and female cells come together and the resulting fertilized cells develop into seeds. Spermatophyes are divided into gymnosperms ('naked seeds') – including cycads, cycadeoids or bennettitales, cordaitales, ginkgos and conifers – and the flowering plants.

Williamsonia

Below: The fronds of Williamsonia are characteristically slender. Like all cycadeoids (the group Bennettitales), they have many small leaflets, or pinnae, alternating on either side of the main stem, or midrib. This pattern is known as the Ptilophyllum type, and differs from cycadales in which the pinnae usually occur in opposite pairs.

Cycads were among the dominant large plants found in the Mesozoic Era. The cycadales include both fossil and living forms, with about a hundred extant species in Mexico, the West Indies, Australia and South Africa, while the cycadeoids (bennettitales) are all extinct. *Williamsonia* is the best-known cycadeoid. The trunk was long and slender (although it could be short and bulbous in other cycadeoids), and the leaves narrow and frond-like. Fossil cycadeoids and cycadales can be distinguished if the leaf cuticle is exceptionally well preserved and cell walls can be seen under the microscope. They are quite different in their reproductive structures. Cycadales (including all living species) produce conifer-like cones, while cycadeoids had flower-like structures that suggest they could have played a part in the origin of true flowering plants, the angiosperms.

Name: *Williamsonia*
Meaning: Honouring W C Williamson (1816–95), surgeon and naturalist
Grouping: Gymnosperm, Cycadophyte, Cycadeoid
Informal ID: Gymnosperm, cycad, cycadeoid
Fossil size: Slab 29cm/11½in across
Reconstructed size: Frond width 6–7cm/2⅖–2¾in; height of whole plant 2m/6½ft
Habitat: Dry uplands
Time span: Early Triassic to Cretaceous, 245–120 million years ago
Main fossil sites: Western Europe, Asia (India)
Occurrence: ◆ ◆

Cycadeoidea

Below: This section of fossilized Cycadeoidea trunk distinctly shows the reproductive structures (or 'buds') embedded just under the surface. These were originally thought to have been precursors to true flower structures, but they are now known to have remained closed in life and so were probably self-pollinated.

Cycadeoidea was one of the most common North American cycadeoids. Its fossils are usually of the short, almost spherical or barrel-shaped trunk that was topped by a crown of fronds. When these trunks are well preserved, several 'buds' can be seen embedded just below the surface. These buds bear many small ovules (containing egg cells) in a central structure, surrounded by filaments bearing pollen sacs with the male cells. It was thought that these buds would later emerge as flower-like structures, but they are now known to have remained closed, and were probably self-pollinated. *Cycadeoidea* was a very common plant in the Cretaceous Period of North America, but it is rarely found elsewhere. The leaf bases are usually preserved covering the trunk, making many of the fossils resemble petrified pineapples.

Name: *Cycadeoidea*
Meaning: Cycad-like
Grouping: Gymnosperm, Cycad, Cycadeoid
Informal ID: Cycadeoid, bennettitale
Fossil size: Slab 15cm/6in high
Reconstructed size: Whole plant height up to 1m/3¼ft
Habitat: Dry uplands
Time span: Jurassic to Cretaceous, 170–110 million years ago
Main fossil sites: North America, Asia (India)
Occurrence: ◆ ◆ ◆ (North America only)

Cycadites

Name: *Cycadites*
Meaning: Related to cycads
Grouping: Gymnosperm, Cycad, possibly Cycadale
Informal ID: Cycad
Fossil size: Slab 8cm/3⅛in wide
Reconstructed size: Whole fronds may exceed 20cm/8in in length
Habitat: Moist to dry forests
Time span: Jurassic to Cretaceous, 180–100 million years ago
Main fossil sites: Worldwide
Occurrence: ◆ ◆ ◆

The fossil leaf *Cycadites* is found in many parts of the world, from the Indian subcontinent through to Scandinavia. Despite its abundance, however, comparatively little is known of *Cycadites* in life. This is because well-preserved fossils of the whole plant are exceptionally rare. The plant seems to be more closely related to the cycadales than to the cycadeoids (bennettitales), as evidenced by the leaflets (pinnae) emerging in opposing pairs from the frond's main stem, or midrib. *Cycadites* is an example of a form-genus – a scientific name that is assigned to a certain part of a plant. As with examples such as *Psaronius* and *Medullosa*, which have been detailed on previous pages, this has resulted in numerous difficulties for researchers and scientists in identifying and naming specimens. Other cycad fragments similar to *Cycadites* include *Pagiophyllum* and *Otozamites* (*Otopteris*).

Right: This fragment of Cycadites *frond has been preserved in red (oxidized) mudstone. The fragment is approximately 12cm/4¾in long. Note the leaflets (pinnae) in opposite pairs. Some species of* Cycadites *are known from Permian times, but most thrived during the Jurassic and Cretaceous Periods.*

Midrib | Pinnae

Zamites

Name: *Zamites*
Meaning: From Zamia
Grouping: Gymnosperm, Cycad, Cycadale
Informal ID: Cycad
Fossil size: Fronds up to 20cm/8in across
Reconstructed size: Height up to 3m/10ft
Habitat: Wide range of terrestrial habitats
Time span: Tertiary, less than 65 million years ago
Main fossil sites: Worldwide
Occurrence: ◆ ◆ ◆

Right: Here a fragment of Zamites *leaf, or frond, has been preserved in red (oxidized) mudstone. The species is* Zamites buchianus *from the Fairlight Clays of Sussex, England. The living* Zamia *has a short, wide, pithy stem topped by leathery fronds.*

Zamites is, like *Cycadites* (above), a form-genus – and its fossil leaf is extremely similar in form to the living cycad genus *Zamia*. Today, *Zamia* is found exclusively in the Americas, its habitat ranging from Georgia, USA, south to Bolivia. *Zamites* and similar forms have been found in places as far apart as France, Alaska and Australia, a pattern which suggests that *Zamia*, or its ancestors, had a much wider geographic distribution in the past. This makes *Zamites* very interesting from the point of view of biogeography, which is the study of the distribution of animals and plants across the planet. The oldest cycad fossils are from the Early Permian of China, some 280 million years ago, and show that cycads have remained virtually unchanged through their long history. In general, a typical cycad looks outwardly like a palm tree or tree fern, with a trunk-like stem that can be either short and bulbous (resembling a pine cone or pineapple) or tall and columnar, crowned by an 'umbrella' of arching evergreen fronds. Cycads have ranged widely in size: some ground-hugging at just 10cm/4in tall; others more tree-like at almost 20m/66ft. Their average height, however, is about 2m/6½ft. Some types are informally called sago palms, although they are not true palms (which are flowering plants, Angiosperma).

Strap-like leathery fronds

Central frond stalk (midrib)

FLOWERING PLANTS (ANGIOSPERMS)

The angiosperms include most flowers, herbs, shrubs, vines, grasses and blossom-producing broadleaved trees. The presence of flowers, and seeds enclosed in fruits (angiosperm means 'seed in receptacle'), differentiate them from gymnosperms, such as conifers. There are two great groups of angiosperms: monocotyledons and dicotyledons. 'Monocot' seeds have one cotyledon, or seed-leaf, in the seed.

Phragmites (reed)

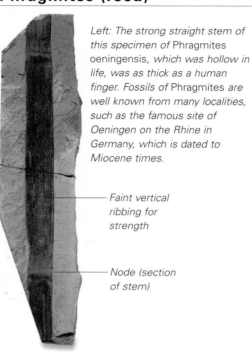

Left: The strong straight stem of this specimen of Phragmites oeningensis, which was hollow in life, was as thick as a human finger. Fossils of Phragmites are well known from many localities, such as the famous site of Oeningen on the Rhine in Germany, which is dated to Miocene times.

Faint vertical ribbing for strength

Node (section of stem)

The genus *Phragmites* is well known today around the world as the common reed or marsh grass *P. australis*. Tall and tough, in some regions it grows higher than 5m/16½ft and its dense, tangled rootstock spreads rapidly. *Phragmites* fringes not only lakes and slow rivers but also brackish water, and is regarded in many areas as an invasive pest. It has stout unbranched stems and long, slim leaves with bases that sheath the stem as it grows. The soft, feathery flower-heads are a shiny purple-brown colour. The dried stems are cut for many purposes, including roof thatching. *Phragmites* fossils are among the most common plant remains in some localities, especially from the Miocene Epoch to recent times. Reeds, grasses and rushes are placed in the large monocotyledon family Gramineae.

Name: *Phragmites*
Meaning: Fence-like growth
Grouping: Angiosperm, Monocotyledon, Graminean
Informal ID: Reed
Fossil size: Specimen height 18cm/7in
Reconstructed size: Plant height 4m/13ft or more
Habitat: Fringing bodies of fresh and brackish water
Time span: Mostly Tertiary, 60 million years ago, to today
Main fossil sites: Worldwide
Occurrence: ◆ ◆

Sabal (palm)

Below: This specimen of a fan-like leaf pattern from Aix-en-Provence, France, dates to the Eocene Epoch. Palm leaves are generally tough and durable (as known from their uses today, such as thatching, wrapping and cooking). They have thickened veins that run side by side, known as parallel venation, which is characteristic of all monocotyledons.

Palm trees (family Palmae or Arecaceae) are familiar in many warmer regions, and are grown for their wood, frond-like leaves and nut-like or juicy seeds that produce oil, starch and other useful materials, as well as providing edible dates and coconuts. A typical palm has an unbranched, almost straight trunk covered with ring-, arc- or scale-like scars where leaf bases were once attached. The trunk cannot grow thicker like most other trees but remains almost the same diameter to the crown of frond-like leaves, which may be fan-like, feathery or fern-like. Palm fossils of genera such as *Sabal* and *Palmoxylon* are known from the Late Cretaceous Period, 80-plus million years ago. By the Early Tertiary Period, 60 million years ago, they were evolving fast, and living genera such as *Phoenix* (date palms) and *Nypa* (mangrove palms) had appeared. There are hundreds of extinct species and more than 2,700 living ones.

Name: *Sabal*
Meaning: Food
Grouping: Angiosperm, Monocotyledon, Palmaean
Informal ID: Palm tree
Fossil size: Specimen length 32cm/12½in
Reconstructed size: Tree height 20–30m/66–100ft
Habitat: Tropics
Time span: Eocene, 50 million years ago
Main fossil sites: Worldwide
Occurrence: ◆ ◆

Bevhalstia

Name: *Bevhalstia*
Meaning: For palaeontologist
L Beverly Halstead
Grouping: Angiosperm
Informal ID: 'Wealden weed'
Fossil size: Stems and
shoots up to 15cm/6in;
flower-like structure 5mm/³⁄₁₆in
across
Reconstructed size: Whole
plant height up to 25cm/10in
Habitat: Freshwater swamps
Time span: Early Cretaceous,
130–125 million years ago
Main fossil sites: Europe
(Southern England)
Occurrence: ◆ ◆

Bevhalstia was possibly one of the first flowering plants to have appeared on the Earth and it dates back to the Early Cretaceous Period, some 130–125 million years ago. The plant had an enigmatic combination of features, with leaves that had a vascular system (tube-like network) similar to those of ferns and mosses, together with angiosperm-like buds and flower-like features. *Bevhalstia* was likely to have been a delicate herbaceous (non-woody) plant. Despite its fragile nature, however, it has been found in abundance in the fossil record, suggesting that it grew very near to its burial sites, which were possibly quiet lakes or swamp bottoms. If this is accurate, then *Bevhalstia* probably had an aquatic way of life, perhaps similar to today's *Cabomba* or fanwort pond and aquarium plants. Some of the first specimens of *Bevhalstia* were collected in the 1990s as part of the studies of the fish-eating dinosaur *Baryonyx* being carried out at London's Natural History Museum.

Right: The flower-like structure of Bevhalstia *is one of the first to appear in the fossil record, in the Early Cretaceous, and it already shows what could be interpreted as 'petals'.*

Above: In this fragment of Bevhalstia *the delicate nature of the stem is a clue to the plant's probable way of life, part-submerged in the manner of modern pondweeds.*

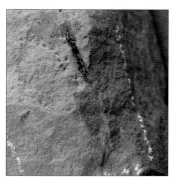

Pabiana

Name: *Pabiana*
Meaning: After Pabian
(see text)
Grouping: Angiosperm,
Dicotyledon, Magnoliacean
Informal ID: Magnolia leaf
Fossil size: Leaf length
5–7cm/2–2¾in
Reconstructed size: Tree
height 10m/33ft plus
Habitat: Warmer forests
Time span: Middle
Cretaceous, 100 million
years ago
Main fossil sites:
North America
Occurrence: ◆ ◆

Pabiana is usually regarded as a Cretaceous member of the magnolias, family Magnoliaceae. These were among the first flowering trees to evolve, in the Early to Middle Cretaceous Period. The group still has about 80–120 living species, mostly distributed in warmer parts of the Americas and Asia. Although many similar flowers are usually associated with pollination by bees, magnolias evolved their large blossoms well before the appearance of bees, and instead they are pollinated by beetles. Because of this, the bloom is quite tough and fossilizes fairly well – that is, compared with other flowers. A primitive aspect of magnolias is their lack of – or combination of, depending on the point of view – distinct petals or sepals. The name 'tepal' has been coined to describe these intermediate structures in magnolias, which look like the petals of other flowers. The original specimens of *Pabiana* were discovered at the Rose Creek Quarry near Fairbury, Nebraska, USA, in 1968 by a team including American palaeontologist Roger K Pabian, who was actually searching for fossil invertebrates. The genus was named after him in 1990.

Right: Leaves of Pabiana *were lanceolate (lance-shaped) and were very similar to those of living magnolias. This specimen is from Middle Cretaceous rocks found in Nebraska, USA.*

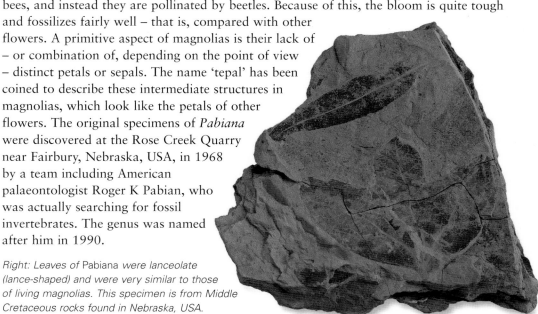

EARLY INVERTEBRATES

The most ancient animal fossils, such as those from Precambrian Ediacara in Australia or the Middle Cambrian Burgess Shale in North America, have received varying interpretations over the years. Some of those life-forms were so different from any others, living or extinct, that the term 'Problematica' is used when precise taxonomic position is uncertain.

Mawsonites

Hand-sized *Mawsonites* are one of the most difficult of the Ediacaran life-forms to interpret with any degree of certainty. With its multi-lobed, expanding radial symmetry – that is, a wheel- or petal-like structure – it has been called almost everything from a flower to an aberrant sea lily (crinoid). However, it comes from a time well before flowering plants had yet evolved. One of the more established theories regarding its origins is that it was some kind of scyphozoan – that is, a jellyfish from the cnidarian group. Its unique features, however, make it difficult to assign to any of the known jellyfish groupings, either those living or extinct. In addition, its surface topography, which has some fairly sharp and well-defined ridges, is not reminiscent of a floppy, jelly-like organism. Another possibility regarding its origins is that the fossils are the remains of a radial burrow system made by some type of creature, perhaps a worm, tunnelling and looking for food in the sandy, silty sea bed of the seas and oceans of the time. This would mean it is a trace fossil – traces left by an organism, rather than preserved parts of the actual organism itself.

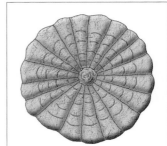

Name: *Mawsonites*
Meaning: Mawson's animal (after Australian Antarctic explorer Sir Douglas Mawson)
Grouping: Animal, Cnidarian, Scyphozoan?
Informal ID: Ediacara 'jellyfish' or trace fossil
Fossil size: Overall width 12–14cm/4¾–5½in
Reconstructed size: Unknown
Habitat: Sea bed
Time span: Precambrian, about 570 million years ago
Main fossil sites: Australia
Occurrence: ◆

Central disc

Innermost set of concentric rings

Outermost lobes

Outer margin

Left: Resembling multiple, expanding whorls of flower petals, the reddish sandstone impression known as Mawsonites *has an overall circular outline composed of curved lobes. The central disc is well defined, with concentric sets of roughly circular raised 'rings' that become more straight-sided towards the outer margin.*

Naraoia

This thumb-size arthropod was at first believed to be some kind of branchiopod crustacean (a cousin of today's water-flea, *Daphnia*). The shiny, two-part covering 'shield', or carapace, bears a central groove from head to tail and a division from side to side into two valves, front and rear. Around the edge of the carapace is a fringe of limb and appendage endings. Dissection into the thickness of the fossil, down through the carapace, has revealed the limbs and appendages in more detail, showing how and where they join to the main body underneath. The results indicated, very unexpectedly, that *Naraoia* was some type of trilobite. However it is not tri-lobed, with left, middle and right sections to the carapace, but rather bi-lobed, with just left and right. Similarly, it has not three divisions from head to tail, but two.

Below: Preservation of Burgess Shale trilobites is exceptional, as some of these are entire animals rather than just shed body casings. Naraoia is an early and unusual trilobite, with front and rear sections to the carapace and one central furrow from head to tail. Comparison of specimens shows that Naraoia may have retained immature features into mature adulthood, a phenomenon known as neoteny.

Name: *Naraoia*
Meaning: From the nearby locally named Narao lakes
Grouping: Arthropod, Trilobite
Informal ID: Early trilobite
Fossil size: Carapace front–rear about 3cm/1⅛in
Reconstructed size: Width 2.5cm/1in, including limbs
Habitat: Sea bed
Time span: Middle Cambrian, 530 million years ago
Main fossil sites: North America
Occurrence: ◆

Burgessia

Named after the shale rocks of its Burgess Pass discovery region in Canada, *Burgessia* was probably some type of bottom-dwelling arthropod. The creature is known from thousands of specimens discovered at the locality. *Burgessia* probably walked, burrowed or swam weakly across the sea floor, and fed mainly by filtering tiny edible particles of food from the general ooze on the ocean floor. Its protective, convex (domed) shield-like carapace was about the size of a fingernail and it covered the softer, vulnerable parts beneath, so that only the ends of the limbs, two antennae-like feelers, which were directed forwards, and the long tail spine were visible from above. In the carapace was a branching set of canals, or grooves, which may have been part of the digestive system. In some specimens the tail spine is twice as long as the body.

Hurdia

The Burgess fossils show the first large-scale evolution of a mineralized, or chitinous, exoskeleton – a hard outer casing, usually found over the top of the body and used for protection as well as muscle anchorage. *Hurdia* has been included in the group known as anomalocarids. Its mouthparts may have had an extra set of teeth within, forming a so-called 'pharyngeal mill' that would be able to grind up other harder-bodied victims – showing that predators were already adapting to well-protected prey.

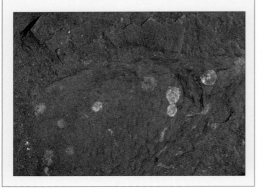

Name: *Burgessia*
Meaning: Of Burgess
Grouping: Arthropod, otherwise uncertain
Informal ID: Burgess arthropod
Fossil size: 1cm/⅜in across
Reconstructed size: Head–tail length 2.5cm/1in
Habitat: Sea bed
Time span: Middle Cambrian, 530 million years ago
Main fossil sites: North America
Occurrence: ◆

Tail section | Main carapace

Tail spine | Head end

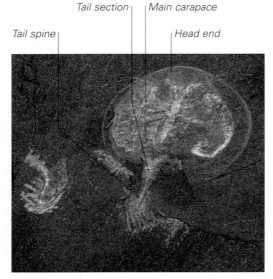

Left: Detailed study of Burgessia *reveals that the body has a cephalic (head) region, about nine main body sections or segments, a telson (tail section) and a long spiny tail. The two antennae were directed so that they pointed forwards. Piecing together the remains of many specimens shows that the creature's 9 or 10 pairs of legs were uniramous (unbranched) and probably bore gills for obtaining oxygen from the water.*

SPONGES

The sponges, phylum Porifera, are strange animals that live permanently rooted to the rocks or mud of the sea bed. They flush water through their porous bodies and filter out tiny food particles. Sponges have an extremely simple anatomy, lacking specialized organs, nerves and muscles and possessing only a few basic cell types. From Cambrian times, most sponges have left plentiful fossils of their mineralized bodies.

Doryderma

Name: *Doryderma*
Meaning: Porous-skinned
Grouping: Poriferan, Demosponge, Lithistid, Megamorinan, Dorydermatid
Informal ID: Doryderma sponge
Fossil size: Specimen 7cm/2¾in high
Reconstructed size: 50cm/20in plus
Habitat: Sea floor
Time span: Carboniferous to Late Cretaceous, 350–85 million years ago
Main fossil sites: Throughout Europe
Occurrence: ◆ ◆

Doryderma is an example of the Demospongea class of sponges – a group that is distinguished by building their skeletons out of both silica spicules and/or a network of tough, cartilage-like fibres of the substance spongin, which is a nitrogenous, hornlike material. Where spicules are present in this class, they are typically both highly complex in shape and capable of meshing together to form a network of significant strength – the skeletons of living demosponges have been observed to hold together long after the death of the animal itself. *Doryderma* is a reasonably common fossil in European marine rocks. However, the atypical branching form that makes it so attractive also makes it prone to damage and fragmentation.

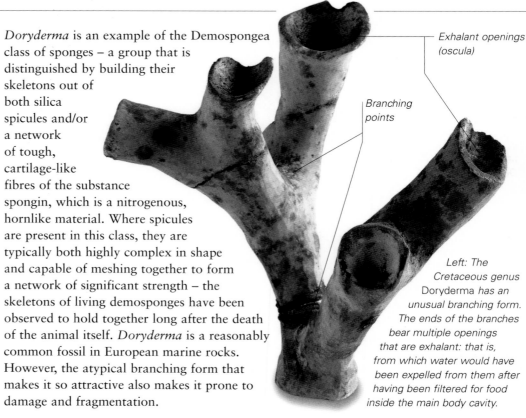

Exhalant openings (oscula)

Branching points

Left: The Cretaceous genus Doryderma has an unusual branching form. The ends of the branches bear multiple openings that are exhalant: that is, from which water would have been expelled from them after having been filtered for food inside the main body cavity.

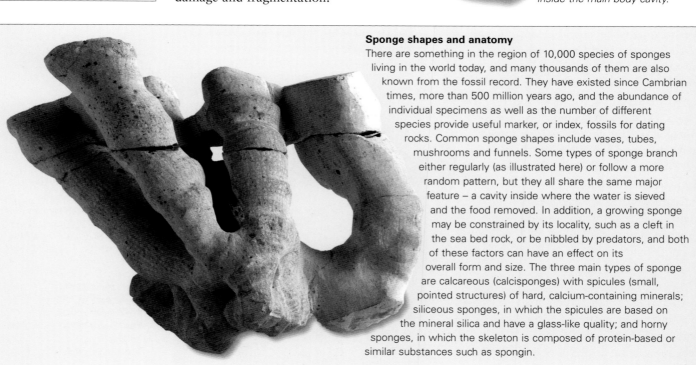

Sponge shapes and anatomy

There are something in the region of 10,000 species of sponges living in the world today, and many thousands of them are also known from the fossil record. They have existed since Cambrian times, more than 500 million years ago, and the abundance of individual specimens as well as the number of different species provide useful marker, or index, fossils for dating rocks. Common sponge shapes include vases, tubes, mushrooms and funnels. Some types of sponge branch either regularly (as illustrated here) or follow a more random pattern, but they all share the same major feature – a cavity inside where the water is sieved and the food removed. In addition, a growing sponge may be constrained by its locality, such as a cleft in the sea bed rock, or be nibbled by predators, and both of these factors can have an effect on its overall form and size. The three main types of sponge are calcareous (calcisponges) with spicules (small, pointed structures) of hard, calcium-containing minerals; siliceous sponges, in which the spicules are based on the mineral silica and have a glass-like quality; and horny sponges, in which the skeleton is composed of protein-based or similar substances such as spongin.

Spongia

Name: *Spongia*
Meaning: Sponge
Classification: Poriferan, Demosponge, Keratosid, Spongiid
Informal ID: Bath sponge
Fossil size: 8cm/3in across
Reconstructed size: Up to 20cm/8in across
Habitat: Sea floor
Time span: Carboniferous, 350 million years ago, to today
Main fossil sites: Worldwide
Occurrence: ◆ ◆

The Spongiidae family includes excellent examples of demosponges, which possess a skeleton composed entirely of branching and interwoven fibres made of spongin. This makes it highly flexible even when dry. The much harder, mineralized, spicule-type elements of the skeleton are almost completely absent. Modern forms of the genus *Spongia* are probably most familiar as the traditional 'bath sponges' of recent years – which are actually the dried corpses of this most 'spongy' of sponges, used for their mild exfoliating properties and ability to absorb water. The fossil record of the Spongiidae shows that these sponges have been a feature of the sea floor at varied depths since the beginnings of the Carboniferous Period.

Right: Spongia *is a fossil from the same group as the modern 'bath sponge'. It possessed a soft, highly flexible skeleton – a feature that often resulted in poor preservation as a fossil. The example shown here is from the Cretaceous Red Chalk of Hunstanton in Norfolk, England.*

Verruculina

Verruculina is a genus of demosponge that lived from the Mid Cretaceous to the Tertiary, chiefly in Europe. The genus possessed a network of spongin reinforced by small, simple spicules embedded in the elastic material (in a similar manner to fibreglass). This gave the whole sponge a skeleton midway in rigidity between those of *Doryderma* and *Spongia*. *Verruculina* did not have an almost fully enclosed central space in the manner of most sponges – with many small, inhalant pores for drawing in water, and one large exhalant pore (the osculum) for pushing the water out. Instead, it possessed a broad, squat body that unfolded at the top, resembling a sprouting leaf or a bracket fungus.

Below: Verruculina *was a distinctive demosponge and it resembles the bracket fungus, which grows on tree trunks. It was once common in the Cretaceous seas that covered Europe – this specimen is Late Cretaceous chalk – but it steadily declined during the Tertiary Period before its eventual extinction.*

Name: *Verruculina*
Meaning: Wart-like
Grouping: Poriferan, Demonsponge, Lithistid, Leiodorellid
Informal ID: Bracket-fungus sponge
Fossil size: 7cm/2¾in across
Reconstructed size: Typically 10cm/4in diameter
Habitat: Sea floor
Time span: Middle Cretaceous to Tertiary, 110–2 million years ago
Main fossil sites: Throughout Europe
Occurrence: ◆ ◆ ◆

ARTHROPODS – TRILOBITES

Arthropods include millions of species that are alive today: insects, arachnids or spiders and scorpions, millipedes or diplopodans, centipedes or chilopodans, and crabs, shrimps and other crustaceans. These are covered in the following pages, starting with the long-extinct trilobites. The uniting feature of arthropods is their hard outer casing and usually numerous jointed limbs. The name means 'joint-foot'.

Anomalocaris

Most creatures of Cambrian times, as revealed by Burgess Shale fossils, were small – generally one to a few centimetres. The arthropods known as anomalocarids, however, commonly grew to 50cm/20in, and some reached almost 2m/6½ft. They were the largest animals of their time. *Anomalocaris* had a disc-like mouth that was originally interpreted as being a separate jellyfish-like animal, known as *Peytoia*. It also had large, strong, forward-facing appendages, which in some species bore sharp spines. These powerful spiked 'limbs', along with large eyes and strong swimming lobes, like paddles along the sides of the body, suggest that *Anomalocaris* was the top predator of its age. It probably fed on soft-bodied animals, such as worms, and perhaps even on trilobites. The relationship of anomalocarids to other arthropods is not yet fully understood (see also *Hurdia*).

Below: This lateral (side) view shows one of the two multi-segmented frontal appendages. Such specimens were originally interpreted as separate shrimp-like creatures, until experts eventually realized that they were detached parts of a larger animal. The small spines on each segment may have assisted in capturing their prey.

Name: *Anomalocaris*
Meaning: Anomalous shrimp
Grouping: Arthropod, Anomalocarid
Informal ID: Anomalocarid, Burgess 'supershrimp'
Fossil size: 7.5cm/3in
Reconstructed size: Total length, including front appendages, 60cm/24in
Habitat: Shallow seas
Time span: Cambrian, 530 million years ago
Main fossil sites: North America (Burgess), Asia (China)
Occurrence: ◆

Cruziana

The name *Cruziana* is used for a trackway, or 'footprints', made by an arthropod filter-feeding in the muddy sea bed. The chevron-like indentations were created as the animal used its limbs to plough into the ooze, stirring the sediment into suspension (floating in the water). While moving the sediment towards its rear end, the animal could filter out edible particles and move them forward towards its mouth. As a trace fossil, or ichnogenus, *Cruziana* refers to a particular type of behaviour and the evidence that results, but not the type of animal that created it. However, it is commonly assumed that some types of trilobites were responsible. In some examples, specimens of *Calymene* (see opposite) have been found at the end of the trackway. But any arthropod feeding or moving in this manner could conceivably be the trackmaker.

Name: *Cruziana*
Meaning: Of Cruz (in honour of General Santa Cruz of Bolivia)
Grouping: Arthropod, trilobite
Informal ID: Cruziana, trilobite trackway
Fossil size: Track width 3cm/1in
Reconstructed size: As above
Habitat: Muddy sea floor
Time span: Cambrian to Permian, 540–250 million years ago
Main fossil sites: Europe, North America, South America, Australia
Occurrence: ◆ ◆ ◆

Left: It is most likely that the trace fossils known as Cruziana were made by trilobite-like creatures. The trackmaker's direction of travel is towards the open end of the V-shapes, left by appendage movement.

Calymene

Name: *Calymene*
Meaning: Stony crescent
Grouping: Arthropod,
Trilobite, Phacopid
Informal ID: Trilobite
Fossil size: 3.2cm/1¼in
Reconstructed size: Unrolled
head–tail length 4cm/1½in
Habitat: Shallow seas
Time span: Silurian to
Devonian, 430–360 million
years ago
Main fossil sites: Europe,
North America
Occurrence: ◆ ◆ ◆ ◆

Calymene was a medium-size trilobite. It was probably a predator and was found in shallow Silurian seas, usually in lagoons or reefs. It had a semicircular-shaped cephalon (head shield) with three or four distinct 'lobes' that ran laterally along its central head section, known as the glabella. The glabella itself was bell-shaped, containing small eyes. There was a variable number of segments (or tergites) in the middle region, the thorax, depending on the species concerned – British specimens, for example, may have up to 19 segments, while those from North American species have only 13. Its tough exoskeleton, like that found on many post-Cambrian trilobites, was a good defence against predation and also increased its own chances of being preserved in the fossil record. This has helped to make *Calymene* one of the most commonly found trilobite genera from the Middle Ordovician Period.

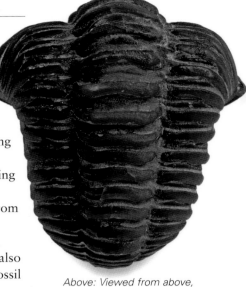

Above: *Viewed from above,* Calymene *shows its segmented main body structure and its almost non-existent pygidium, or tail.*

Right: This is a three-quarter front view of a partially enrolled Calymene. *The ability of many trilobites to roll up is thought to be a defence against predators attacking the unprotected underside.*

Right: In front view, the cephalon of Calymene blumenbachii *was more triangular, compared with the rounded cephalon of most other trilobite groups.*

Diacalymene

Name: *Diacalymene*
Meaning: Through Calymene
Grouping: Arthropod,
Trilobite, Phacopid
Informal ID: Trilobite
Fossil size: Head–tail
length 5cm/2in
Reconstructed size:
As above
Habitat: Shallow seas
Time span: Silurian to
Devonian, 430–360 million
years ago
Main fossil sites: Europe,
North America
Occurrence: ◆ ◆ ◆ ◆

Diacalymene is closely related to *Calymene*, to the point where some palaeontologists have suggested that they should be regarded as the same genus. However, there are some differences between the two. For a start, *Diacalymene* has a distinct ridge along the anterior of the cephalon, as well as a narrower glabella (central head region) than *Calymene*. In addition, *Diacalymene* also has a slightly more triangular-shaped cephalon (head shield), and it also tended to live in muddier sediments than did *Calymene*. Like *Calymene*, however, *Diacalymene* could roll up tightly for protection against threats, such as predators and storms.

Right: This large and complete fossilized specimen of Diacalymene *was discovered in a trilobite-rich formation in an area known as the Laurence Uplift, Oklahoma, USA.*

MOLLUSCS – BIVALVES

The bivalve molluscs known as oysters are characterized by their tendency to encrust rocks and other shells. Oysters are useful 'way-up' indicators. This is because they lie encrusted on one valve, so the other exposed, upward-facing valve acts as a hard surface for its own smaller encrustations such as barnacles. This indicates which way up the oyster – and often fossils associated with it – were in life.

Lopha

The lifestyle and habitat of ancient bivalves are usually derived from analogy to their living relations. The shell shape and form of oysters such as *Lopha*, *Ostrea* and *Rastellum* are often highly irregular and reflect the shape of the surface on which that particular individual grew. In many cases the external features of oyster shells are so variable that recognizing the various species is very difficult, especially among mixed assemblages. As a general rule, internal features, such as muscle scars, are more reliable for identification. Oysters possess only one adductor muscle, which produces large and distinct muscle scars where it attaches to the inside of the valves. A much smaller pair of muscles, the Quenstedt muscles, attach to the gills and leave small muscle scars.

Above: Jurassic Lopha marshi *(Ostrea marshii) grew in a variety of shapes, partly determined by the room available. The curled shape and prominent V-like ridges have led to the common name of coxcomb oyster.*

Left: Lopha marshi *often lived among hardground communities where ageing, lithified sediments were exposed on the sea floor, giving a weathered, cement-like substrate.*

Name: *Lopha*
Meaning: Crested, peaked
Grouping: Mollusc, Bivalve
Informal ID: Oyster, coxcomb (cock's comb) oyster
Fossil size: 6–7cm/2½in
Reconstructed size: Less than 10cm/4in
Habitat: Shallow sea floor
Time span: Late Jurassic to Late Cretaceous, 160–70 million years ago
Main fossil sites: Europe, Asia
Occurrence: ◆ ◆

Gryphaeostrea

Below: The flattened attachment surface present on one of these oysters suggests that they were attached to a large aragonite bivalve, which has not been preserved.

Attachment surface

Most mollusc shells are calcareous, which means that they are built from calcium carbonate minerals. There are two main forms of calcium carbonate: calcite and aragonite. Aragonite is less robust than calcite, and often dissolves away during fossilization. Oysters form their shells from calcite, but many of the groups that they encrust, such as cephalopods, gastropods and other bivalves, have shells formed of aragonite. The result is that fossil oysters are often found apparently unattached, because the shells they were encrusting have not been preserved. However, the encrusting surface of the oyster represents a very faithful mould showing the shape of the surface it was once attached to – often sufficiently detailed for the former host to be identified.

Name: *Gryphaeostrea*
Meaning: Grabber oyster
Grouping: Mollusc, Bivalve
Informal ID: Oyster
Fossil size: 4cm/1½in
Reconstructed size: Up to 10cm/4in
Habitat: Hard objects, such as shell or bone, found on the sea floor
Time span: Cretaceous to Miocene, 115–10 million years ago
Main fossil sites: Worldwide
Occurrence: ◆ ◆ ◆

Gryphea

Name: Gryphea
Meaning: Grabber
Grouping: Mollusc, Bivalve
Informal ID: Oyster, 'devil's toenails'
Fossil size: Specimen lengths 7–10cm/2¾–4in
Reconstructed size: As above
Habitat: Sea floor
Time span: Late Triassic to Late Jurassic, 220–140 million years ago
Main fossil sites: Worldwide
Occurrence: ◆ ◆ ◆ ◆

Various forms of *Gryphea* were among the first true oysters, appearing in the Triassic Period. The tiny free-moving larva, or 'spat', attached to a small particle (rather than a large rock) as its initial hard substrate. It soon outgrew this, however, and became essentially free-living, reclined on the sea floor. Like other bivalves, the valves of the oyster shell are on either side of the animal (even though one usually faces up and the other down) and can be referred to as the left and right valves. For true oysters which encrust, the left valve attaches to the hard substrate. In the free-living adult *Gryphea* the left valve is large and coiled while the right valve is more like a small cap. In life, the animal would have rested on the left valve with the right valve facing upwards. The thick plug of calcite around the umbo (the original, first-formed, beak-like part) of the left valve acted as a counterbalance to keep the opening between the valves raised above the sediment. Many types of *Gryphea* were very successful through the Mesozoic Era.

Pearls

Oysters are famed for containing pearls. These are generated as a defensive substance to 'wall off' particles that enter the shell and irritate the animal. This process can be simulated artificially by inserting shell fragments into farmed oysters. Pearls are sometimes found preserved in fossil oysters. However, the usual mineral replacement, which is part of fossilization, has taken place, and so the pearly lustrous appearance has long been lost.

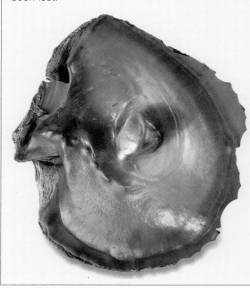

Left: Gryphea *oysters usually show pronounced growth ridges, as the valves of the shell grew seasonally at their widening edges, or margins. Fossils of these early oysters are common enough finds to have entered into folklore – their talon-like shape has earned them the nickname of 'devil's toenails'.*

Thick inrolled umbo (first-formed part of valve), acting as a counterbalance

Cap-like right valve

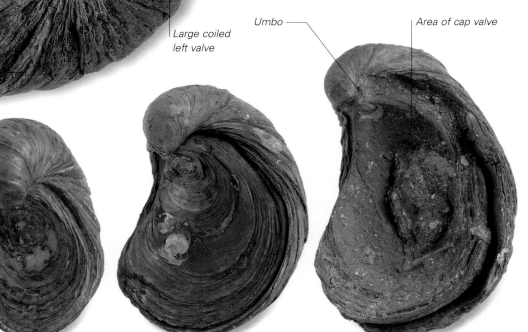

Growth ridges

Large coiled left valve

Umbo

Area of cap valve

Right: Gryphea *of the Early Jurassic display changes in time whereby the left, or coiled, valve becomes broader and more flattened, while the right, or cap, valve becomes larger and more concave. This gave the animals an overall bowl-like appearance, perhaps representing an adaptation to the sediment on which they were living.*

MOLLUSCS – AMMONITES

Ammonites were at their most diverse during the Mesozoic, which corresponds roughly on land to the Age of Reptiles and especially dinosaurs. Ammonites have been extensively studied and are so well known that they are often used as symbols of the fossil record. They are particularly important as index fossils used to identify geologic periods because of their widespread distribution and rapid evolution.

Austiniceras

Faintly S-shaped interval ribs

Flattened sides

Rounded venter

Light intermediate ribs

Relatively evolute (loose-coiled) shell

Ammonites ranged from smaller than a fingernail, even when fully grown, to as large as a dining table. *Austiniceras* was one of the bigger types, with some specimens more than 2.5m/8¼ft across. It is a relatively rare find from the Late Cretaceous Period, mainly in Britain and other European sites. *Austiniceras* has an evolute spiral shell, which may be smooth or lightly ribbed, with slightly more pronounced interval ribs. Its sides are almost flat or gently convex. The narrowly rounded venter suggests that it led an active swimming lifestyle despite its great size.

Left: This small specimen of Austiniceras austeni, *from the Late Cretaceous Lower Chalk of Sussex, England, is about 15cm/6in in diameter. But examples of* Austiniceras *have been known to grow to more than 2m/6½ft across. The generally flattened shell shape (from side to side), low ribs and narrowly rounded venter suggest an active lifestyle, 'jetting' through the water in the manner of a modern squid.*

Name: *Austiniceras*
Meaning: Austin's horn
Grouping: Mollusc, Cephalopod, Ammonoid, Ammonite
Informal ID: Ammonite
Fossil size: 15cm/6in across
Reconstructed size: Some specimens exceed 2m/6½ft in diameter
Habitat: Shallow seas
Time span: Late Cretaceous, 95–70 million years ago
Main fossil sites: Throughout Europe
Occurrence: ◆ ◆

Dactylioceras

Snakes of the sea
Evolute ammonites were once believed to be coiled snakes turned to stone. The shell opening was often carved to resemble a snake's head. The fossils were then sold to pilgrims as serpents that had been petrified by a local saint.

Dactylioceras is a common find in Jurassic bituminous shales. These shales formed when limited water circulation allowed stagnant (still, oxygen-poor) conditions to develop in dense sediments on the sea floor. This was favourable for preservation of ammonites and other shells in various ways. The impermeable nature of the sediment prevented the shell's structure of aragonite material from dissolving away. In addition, the stagnant conditions encountered by the shells when they sank to the bottom meant that burrowing animals or currents would not disturb them as the fossilization process occurred. Several individuals are preserved in the block shown here, discovered in Germany. This suggests that *Dactylioceras* had gregarious (group-living) habits. Possibly, like many modern cephalopods, such as squid, they congregated in large swarms or schools to breed.

Name: *Dactylioceras*
Meaning: Finger horn
Grouping: Mollusc, Cephalopod, Ammonoid, Ammonite
Informal ID: Ammonite
Fossil size: Slab length 15cm/6in
Reconstructed size: Individuals 2–5cm/ ¾–2in across
Habitat: Open sea
Time span: Early Jurassic, 200–175 million years ago
Main fossil sites: Worldwide
Occurrence: ◆ ◆ ◆

Left: The shell of Dactylioceras *is evolute in form, rather than the larger whorls enveloping the smaller, older ones. The ribs branch towards the outside of the whorls to give a braid-edge effect.*

Hamites

Name: *Hamites*
Meaning: Hook-like
Grouping: Mollusc, Cephalopod, Ammonoid, Ammonite
Informal ID: Uncoiled or heteromorph ammonite
Fossil size: Length 6cm/2⅓in
Reconstructed size: Length 8cm/3⅛in
Habitat: Relatively deep sea floor
Time span: Middle Cretaceous, 110–100 million years ago
Main fossil sites: Africa, Eurasia, North America
Occurrence: ◆ ◆ ◆

Not all ammonites or ammonoids have the familiar coiled or spiral shell form that is seen in so many specimens. *Hamites* is a heteromorph, or uncoiled type. It lived alongside *Euhoplites* (see below) in a soft-bottom marine community that has been preserved in detail in Gault Clay, found in Kent, England. In addition to ammonite specimens, other molluscs discovered in the Gault Clay include nautiloids, such as *Eutrephoceras*; gastropods, such as *Nummocalcar* (which is superficially ammonite-like); and the carnivorous snail *Gyrodes* (which fed on the abundant bivalves by boring small circular holes in their shells with its specialized file-like 'tongue', or radula). Other creatures found at this English site include echinoderms, such as the crinoid *Nielsenicrinus*, and crustaceans, such as the lobster *Hoploparia*. (See also *Macroscaphites* on the following page.)

Below: This is a section of the heteromorph ammonite Hamites, *from the Gault Clay of Folkestone in Kent, south-eastern England. It is an internal mould, showing the pattern of joint, or suture, lines on the shell's inner surface. Many Gault Clay specimens of the actual shells retain their original aragonitic material and still show the nacreous 'mother-of-pearl' lustre.*

Younger end (nearer aperture)

— Suture moulds —

Euhoplites

Name: *Euhoplites*
Meaning: Good Hoplite (a heavily armoured ancient Greek soldier), from the related genus *Hoplites*
Grouping: Mollusc, Cephalopod, Ammonoid, Ammonite
Informal ID: Ammonite
Fossil size: 3cm/1¼in across
Reconstructed size: As above
Habitat: Probably sea floor
Time span: Middle Cretaceous, 110–100 million years ago
Main fossil sites: Throughout Europe
Occurrence: ◆ ◆ ◆

Euhoplites is a strongly ribbed example of an ammonite, with the ribs giving way to tubercles (lumps) on the inside of the curvature and with a double-row of ribs around the outside at the venter (the external convex, or 'belly' part, of the shell). *Euhoplites* is a common ammonite in the Gault Clay of Folkestone, as described above for *Hamites*. From the assemblage of fossils, experts can describe a community of animals that lived together and were preserved in their original environment – a relatively deep, calm marine location. *Euhoplites* lived alongside other ammonites, such as the tiny *Hysteroceras*, just 1.8cm/¾in in diameter, as well as *Hamites*. Other animals preserved include the belemnite *Neohibolites*, and there is also evidence for sharks in the form of fossil sharks' teeth.

Right: Euhoplites *is almost pentagonal (five-sided) in cross-section and slightly evolute, with a distinctive deep and narrow ventral groove. As with most ammonites, the creature itself lived in the last-formed, largest chamber and could withdraw into this for safety. The pronounced ribs probably helped to strengthen the shell against predator attack, but they would have caused drag, reducing swimming speed.*

Strong ribs

Inner tubercles

Inflated (rapidly widening) form

Ventral groove between tubercles

Offset double row of keel tubercles

FISH – SHARKS

The sharks were among the very earliest groups of fish, and their sleek, streamlined body design has changed little throughout their long history. Sharks and their close cousins the rays are together known as elasmobranchs and, like other fish, have an internal skeleton. This skeleton is unusual, however, as it is made of the tough, gristly substance known as cartilage, rather than bone, giving them and chimaeras, or ratfish, the name of cartilaginous fish (Chondrichthyes). Cartilage degrades more rapidly than bone after death, so most of our knowledge about prehistoric sharks comes from their well-preserved, abundant teeth and fin spines. These date back to the Early Silurian Period, more than 420 million years ago.

Hybodus

Name: *Hybodus*
Meaning: Healthy, strong tooth
Grouping: Fish, Chondrichthyean, Elasmobranch, Selachian, Hybodontiform
Informal ID: Shark
Fossil size: Length 16cm/6½in (partly complete)
Reconstructed size: Head to tail length up to 2.5m/8¼ft
Habitat: Oceans
Time span: Late Permian to Cretaceous, 260–70 million years ago
Main Fossil sites: Worldwide
Occurrence: ◆ ◆

Below: This dorsal fin spine is probably from Hybodus. *The portion that attached to the body is on the right. It is likely that the spine was partly embedded in the flesh of the fin for about half of its length, with the pointed end projecting freely as a deterrent.*

Hybodus is one of the best-known representatives of a group of smallish, highly successful sharks that ranged from the Late Permian and Early Triassic Periods, some 250 million years ago, to the great end-of-Cretaceous mass extinction 65 million years ago. *Hybodus* grew to more than 2m/6½ft in length and, compared with many of today's modern sharks, it had a bluntish snout. Apart from this, however, it was similar in shape to its living cousins and belonged to the modern shark group, Selachii. It may have had a varied diet, suggested by two types of teeth. The sharp teeth at the front of the mouth were for gripping and slicing slippery prey, such as fish and squid, while the larger, molar-type teeth at the rear of the jaws were perhaps designed for crushing hard-shelled food, such as shellfish. Attached to the front of each of its two dorsal (back) fins was a spine that may well have served as a defence to deter predators that were larger than itself. The spines are the body parts most commonly found as fossils.

Shark jaws

Like the rest of a shark's skeleton, the animal's cartilaginous jaws were rarely preserved. Decomposition of the springy cartilage occurred readily following death, but rare examples of jaw preservation, such as the example below, show teeth in their position in life. Teeth grew continuously behind those in use, and gradually moved to the edge of the jaw. As the teeth at the front were broken off or wore away, the younger teeth moved forward to replace them.

Below: Several rows of teeth formed an effective way of holding and slicing soft, slippery prey, such as fish and squid. Most shark teeth are either triangular in general shape, with a straight base fixed to the jaw, or have a tall, dagger-like central point growing from a low base. The tooth itself is slim, like a blade, and often has tiny saw-like serrations along its exposed cutting edges.

Oldest row of teeth in use

Length around curve of jaw 10cm/4in

Central point of tooth

Base of tooth

Ptychodus

Name: *Ptychodus*
Meaning: Folded tooth
Grouping: Fish,
Chondrichthyean,
Elasmobranch, Selachian,
Hybodontiform
Informal ID: Shark
Fossil size: Single tooth
6cm/2⅜in across; slab
20cm/8in across
Reconstructed size:
Head–tail length up to 3m/10ft
Habitat: Shallow seas
Time span: Cretaceous,
120–70 million years ago
Main fossil sites: Worldwide,
especially North America
Occurrence: ◆ ◆ ◆

Not all sharks had razor-sharp teeth like blades or daggers. *Ptychodus*, for example, possessed large, ribbed, flattened crushing teeth. Hundreds of these teeth were arranged in parallel interlocking rows to form a plate-like grinding surface in the mouth. This form of dentition suggests that such sharks fed chiefly on hard-shelled invertebrates, such as crustaceans and ammonites. Associated fossils show that *Ptychodus* probably lived in shallow marine conditions, and while it attained a worldwide distribution, its remains are particularly abundant in the states of Texas and Kansas, USA.

Below right: Identified as the species Ptychodus polygyrus, *this tooth close-up shows the slightly convex (domed) main biting surface as a row of ridges surrounded by lower lumps, or tubercles. The whole tooth is roughly rectangular in shape.*

Left: Following the animal's death, the tooth plate broke up, creating a jumble of separated, or disarticulated, elements. The different sizes of teeth came from different parts of the grinding tooth plate within the mouth. These teeth have been identified as the species Ptychodus mammillaris *from the Late Cretaceous Period.*

Shark vertebrae

Vertebrae are sometimes called 'backbones', but in sharks they are cartilage like the rest of the skeleton. However, some shark vertebrae may have deposits of hardened, mineralized material similar to true bone, formed by a process known as ossification. Shark vertebrae can usually be recognized by the circular centrum, or main 'body', and the ringed appearance – almost like an animal version of a sectioned tree trunk. This example is 11cm/4⅜in in diameter.

Margin of crown

Coarse ridges

Tubercles (pimple-like lumps)

Convex biting surface

Fish coprolites

Coprolites, or fossilized droppings (faeces), are important for determining the diet of extinct animals. The remains of creatures eaten by sharks, such as shell fragments, bones and scales, can be preserved within the coprolite, showing exactly what these prehistoric creatures were eating. Shark coprolites often take on the spiral or helical pattern of a part of the shark's digestive tract (intestine) called the spiral valve, making them look like pine cones or squat corkscrews.

Below: Shark coprolite, or enterospirae, Late Cretaceous, length 6cm/2⅜in.

Left: Fish coprolite, Triassic, length 2.5cm/1in.

BIRDS

The first known bird is Archaeopteryx, *dating to the Late Jurassic Period, 155–150 million years ago. During the Cretaceous, several further groups of birds appeared, but most died out with the dinosaurs. The only survivor is the Neornithes, to which all present-day 9,000-plus species belong. Bird fossils are rare because their bones were lightweight, fragile and hollow, and were soon scavenged or weathered.*

Archaeopteryx

Among the world's most prized and precious fossils are those of *Archaeopteryx*, the earliest bird so far discovered. Its remains come only from the Solnhofen region of Bavaria, Germany. There, the very fine-grained Lithographic Sandstone (so named because it was formerly quarried for printing) has preserved amazing details, including the patterns of feathers, which are very similar to those of modern flying birds. *Archaeopteryx* had dinosaurian features, such as teeth in its jaws and bones in its tail, but also bird features, including proper flight feathers (rather than fuzzy or downy ones). It probably evolved from small, meat-eating dinosaurs called maniraptorans or 'raptors', but it was perhaps a side-branch of evolution and left no descendants.

Right: One of only seven known fossils of Archaeopteryx, this is termed the 'London specimen'. The neck is arched over its back, a common death pose for reptiles, birds and mammals. The wings show their spread feathers and the legs were strong, with three weight-bearing toes on each foot.

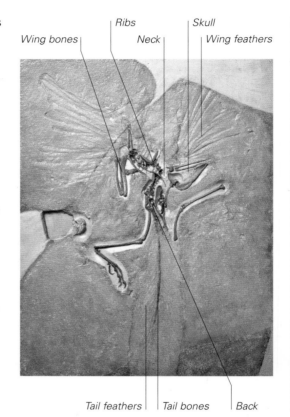

Wing bones | Ribs | Skull
Neck | Wing feathers
Tail feathers | Tail bones | Back

Name: *Archaeopteryx*
Meaning: Ancient wing
Grouping: Aves, Archaeornithes
Informal ID: First bird, early bird
Fossil size: Total width 30cm/12in
Reconstructed size: Nose–tail length 50–60cm/20–24in
Habitat: Wooded areas, tropical islands
Time span: Late Jurassic Period, 155–150 million years ago
Main fossil sites: Europe
Occurrence: ◆

Phalacrocorax

Freshwater and marine birds, such as ducks, geese, gulls, cormorants and waders, are more likely to be preserved than many woodland species, whose remains were quickly scavenged or rotted. A bird that falls into water may quickly be covered by current-borne sand, mud or other sediments. This keeps away oxygen so that aerobic decomposition cannot occur, but fossilization can. Many bird fossils are of species that live around lakes or along seashores. This specimen belongs to the same genus, *Phalacrocorax*, as modern cormorants and shags.

Humerus
Wrist
Hand
Keel
Fingers
Radius and ulna

Left: The cormorant has powerful wing bones for swimming underwater after its food, and a long, hook-tipped, sharp-edged beak for grabbing slippery prey, such as fish.

Name: *Phalacrocorax*
Meaning: Finger raven
Grouping: Aves, Pelicaniform
Informal ID: Cormorant
Fossil size: Beak–tailbone length 60cm/24in
Reconstructed size: Beak–tail length 80cm/32in
Habitat: Seashores, inland waters
Time span: Tertiary Period, Pliocene Epoch, about 2 million years ago
Main fossil sites: Worldwide
Occurrence: ◆

Feathers, nests, eggs and prints

Bird nests and footprints have been preserved as trace fossils in many parts of the world. This process may also occur with the nesting ground burrows of birds such as penguins, and tree holes, such as those made by woodpeckers. The nest shown below is still complete with its eggshells. It may have been raided by a predator or suffered some other sudden catastrophe just after the young hatched, since the empty shells are usually removed by the parent bird or trampled into fragments by the hatchlings. Moulted feathers are another relatively common fossil find for birds, having been shed, fallen into shallow freshwater or marine sediments and then quickly been buried to prevent decomposition. This tends to happen in habitats with still or slow-flowing water, where the sediments are less disturbed.

Above: These trace fossils of bird footprints, from Utah, USA, date to the Eocene Epoch, 53–33 million years ago. They were probably made by a presbyoniform, an early type of bird related to the duck and goose group, Anseriformes. Presbyornis itself looked like a combination of duck and flamingo, and stood 1m/3¼ft tall.

Below: This nest is a pseudofossil – a relatively recent specimen that has become infiltrated and mineralized (petrified, or 'turned to rock') due to the action of water, probably from a splashing spring in a limestone area. It is the typical cup-shaped nest of a small songbird, perhaps in the tit family. The nest diameter is 8cm/3⅛in.

Left: Moulted feathers were often preserved in the fine sediments of lake mud, such as this one from the Oligocene Epoch, about 25 million years ago. Feather width 2cm/¾in.

— *Separated barbs*

Below: Preserved examples of bird eggs include those from waterfowl, such as ducks and geese. Their nests are usually built low, just above the water's surface, and the eggs may fall in and down into the soft, muddy bottom intact if a predator upsets the nest. This may be a duck's egg from the Oligocene Epoch about 25 million years ago. Length 4.5cm/1¾in.

EARLY MAMMALS

*The first mammals appeared almost alongside the first dinosaurs, more than 200 million years ago.
However, throughout the Mesozoic Era they were mostly small, vaguely shrew-like hunters of insects and
other small creatures. Only a few of them exceeded the size of a modern domestic cat, one being
the recently discovered koala-sized Repenomamus.*

Megazostrodon

*Below: This fossil specimen shows the main body or
trunk region with the pelvis (hip) bone, rear limb and
foot bones. In overall appearance, Megazostrodon
and other very early mammals probably looked like
the tree-shrews or tupaids of today, although they
belonged to a very different mammal group, the
triconodonts, which all became extinct.*

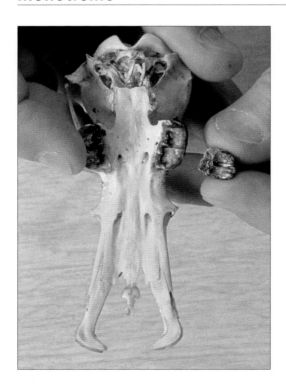

Tibia (shin)

Femur
(thigh)

Vertebrae
(backbones)

Pelvis   Foot bones

One of the earliest known mammals is
Megazostrodon, the remains of which are
known from Late Triassic rocks in Southern
Africa. Around the same time, similar small
mammals were appearing on other
continents. When studying fossils, the key
features of a mammal include the bones that
form the lower jaw (dentary/mandible)
and the jaw joint, and the alteration
of what were formerly jaw bones
to the three tiny bones, called
auditory ossicles, in each
middle ear. Large eye sockets
indicate *Megazostrodon* was
nocturnal, at a time when
the day-active dinosaurs
were beginning to dominate
life on land. Its teeth show it
probably hunted insects in the
manner of today's shrews.

Name: *Megazostrodon*
Meaning: Large
girdle tooth
Grouping: Mammal,
Triconodont
Informal ID: Early mammal,
shrew-like mammal
Fossil size: 3cm/1¼in
Reconstructed size:
Nose–tail length 12cm/4¾in
Habitat: Wooded areas,
scrub regions
Time span: Late Triassic to
Early Jurassic, 210–190
million years ago
Main fossil sites: Regions of
southern Africa
Occurrence: ◆

Monotreme

Today there are just a handful of monotremes
(egg-laying mammals), including the
duck-billed platypus, *Ornithorhynchus*, of
Australia, and the echidnas (spiny anteaters),
Tachyglossus and *Zaglossus*, of Australia
and New Guinea. Of all living mammal
groups, the monotremes have the most
ancient fossil record, stretching back
100 million years. The living platypus shows
reptilian traits, such as limbs angled almost
sideways from the body, and of course egg
laying. However, its defining mammal
features include its three middle ear bones,
warm-bloodedness, a fur-covered body and
feeding its young on milk.

*Left: A monotreme fossil molar tooth is compared
with the teeth in a skull of a modern duck-billed
platypus, Ornithorhynchus. There is great similarity
in the cusp (point) pattern. The fossil tooth is dated
to 63 million years ago, just after the mass extinction
at the end of the Cretaceous Period.*

Name: *Ornithorhynchus*
(living platypus)
Meaning: Bird beak or bill
Grouping: Mammal,
Monotreme
Informal ID: Platypus
Fossil size: Fossil tooth
1cm/⅜in across
Reconstructed size:
Unknown, possible
head–body length 50cm/20in
Habitat: Unknown, possibly
fresh water
Time span: Early Tertiary,
65–60 million years ago
Main fossil sites: (This
specimen) South America;
Australia
Occurrence: ◆

Diprotodon

About one-fifteenth of all living mammal species are marsupials, or pouched mammals, with the biggest being the red kangaroo of Australia. Many other species lived during the Tertiary and Quaternary Periods. One of the largest was *Diprotodon*, which became extinct relatively recently, perhaps just 30,000 years ago. It was a plant-eater resembling a wombat, with a large snout and stocky body. But it was huge, almost the size of a hippo. The protruding nasal area may have supported very large nostrils or the muscles for an elongated snout or shortish, mobile trunk, similar to the modern tapir. Various diprotodontids came and went from the Oligocene Epoch onwards, and their living relations include the wombats themselves, as well as kangaroos and koalas.

Below: An important distinguishing feature of the diprotodonts, as seen in this fossilized skull, was a single pair of lower front incisor teeth, which pointed forwards, and from which the name is derived. There was also a long gap, or diastema, as seen in rodents living today, between the front teeth and rear chewing teeth.

Name: *Diprotodon*
Meaning: Two prominent/forward teeth
Grouping: Mammal, Marsupial, Diprotodont
Informal ID: Giant wombat
Fossil size: Skull length 50cm/20in
Reconstructed size: Head–body length 3m/10ft
Habitat: Woods, forests
Time span: Pleistocene to 30,000 years ago
Main fossil sites: Australia
Occurrence: ◆ ◆

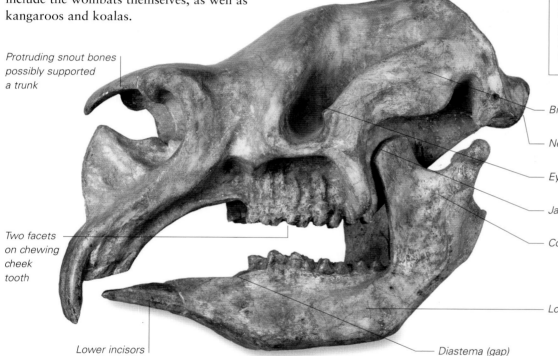

Protruding snout bones possibly supported a trunk

Two facets on chewing cheek tooth

Lower incisors

Brain case

Neck joint

Eye orbit (socket)

Jaw joint

Coronoid process

Lower jaw (mandible)

Diastema (gap)

Protungulatum

The ungulates are the hoofed mammals, which today include horses, rhinos, giraffes, hippos, deer, cattle, sheep and goats. One of the earliest examples was *Protungulatum*. Its fossils have been associated with those of dinosaurs. But the dinosaur fossils from the end of the Mesozoic Era may have been eroded from earlier rocks and then mixed with *Protungulatum*'s remains during the start of the Tertiary Period, about 60 million years ago. *Protungulatum* may have had claw-like 'hooves', but very few remains of this animal are known, other than teeth, which show the trend towards the broad, crushing teeth of later ungulates, designed to masticate tough, fibrous plant foods.

Right: This tiny tooth is from the Hell Creek Formation of Montana, USA. It has two larger pointed cusps, a broken section where other cusps would have stood, and a double-root anchored in the jaw bone. Protungulatum probably fed on fruits and soft plants, but could still chew small creatures, such as insects, as its ancestors had done.

Cusps

Root

Root

Name: *Protungulatum*
Meaning: Before ungulates
Grouping: Mammal, Condylarth
Informal ID: Early hoofed mammal
Fossil size: 5mm/³⁄₁₆in
Reconstructed size: Nose–tail length 40cm/16in
Habitat: Woodland
Time span: Late Cretaceous, 70–65 million years ago, or early Tertiary (see main text)
Main fossil sites: Regions of North America
Occurrence: ◆

INDEX